Who's
Looking
Out
for
You?

ALSO BY BILL O'REILLY

*The O'Reilly Factor: The Good, the Bad,
and the Completely Ridiculous in American Life*

*The No Spin Zone: Confrontations with the
Powerful and Famous in America*

Those Who Trespass: A Novel

BILL O'REILLY

Who's Looking Out for You?

BROADWAY BOOKS | *New York*

The Library of Congress has cataloged the hardcover edition as follows:
O'Reilly, Bill.
Who's looking out for you? / Bill O'Reilly.—1st. ed.
p. cm.
1. United States—Politics and government—2001. 2. United States—
Social conditions—1980. 3. Mass media—Social aspects—United States.
4. Social values—United States. 5. O'Reilly, Bill. I. Title.
B902.07 18 2003
973.931—dc21
2003056084

ISBN 0-7679-1380-9

1 3 5 7 9 10 8 6 4 2

This book is dedicated to Roger Ailes,
who made it all happen.

Contents

Who's Looking Out for You?

Introduction

It ain't me, it ain't me,

I ain't no millionaire's son.

—*John Fogerty, "Fortunate Son"*

LET'S IMMEDIATELY TEE off a few sensitive souls out there by beginning with some "racial profiling." Here goes: If you have started to read this book, the chances are that you're an independent type, but your skin color and ethnicity are not predictable. I don't actually know you, but I know a lot *about* you. That's because there's a certain profile that O'Reilly watchers, listeners, and readers fit most of the time. Sure, there are drive-by viewers who watch *The O'Reilly Factor* as they would a gruesome accident, fascinated but repelled at the same time. And there are snobs who tune in just to shake their heads over the boorishness of it all.

But the everyday American who understands what the Factor concept is all about is generally a person who wants to live life honestly and make his or her own way. That person is often responsible, generous, aware that others around them also have lives to live, and unabashedly patriotic. You, very likely, are one of those people.

In the beginning of the show, the fall of 1996, the elite media tried to marginalize the Factor concept by assigning it a "conservative" label. That's how they tagged us, hoping that label would frighten away those not on the right. But as millions of Americans of all political persuasions watched on television and read my first two books, *The O'Reilly Factor* and *The No Spin Zone,* the establishment press fled, dazed and confused. How could a cable TV news show have such a robust impact when network TV news was losing audience every quarter? The so-called elite scribes couldn't figure it out, and they still can't.

The warfare between the folks who liked *The Factor* and the eggheads in the press who looked down upon it became quite intense at times, but finally the numbers got too big. Millions of Americans tuned in daily to watch and also listen on the radio, causing many in the media to finally wave the white flag. The American people had made *The O'Reilly Factor* into a powerful entity—and the momentum the folks provided resulted in *The Factor* being nominated by the American Television Critics Association for Outstanding Achievement in News and Information in 2002. In 2003 your humble correspondent, me, was chosen by the industry magazine *Television Week* as the second most powerful person in TV news! Yikes! (The NBC news chief, Neil Shapiro, was first.)

So now it's time for me to try to give you something more concrete than a big thank-you. This book is an attempt to zero in on one of the most important parts of life: the ability to recognize who really cares about you as a person—and who does not. If you can master the art of determining that, your life will be much happier and probably much longer. If you fail to understand who is looking out for you, get a good lawyer right now. You're going to need one.

Trust-fund babies and corporate weasels are not allowed to read this book. If you try, I will find out and come to your house, thereby ruining your phony reputation. I will seize your copy of the book and mock you for disobeying the rules. Why would a child of privilege need to waste time with my words? You don't need anyone looking out for you—because you have resources and power already. This book is for everyday Americans who are fighting the good fight.

If you are in this category, here's my first piece of advice: You must learn to become a problem solver, not a problem creator. Problems are one of the few things in life that one can count on. Enough problems will find you so that you do not need to drag unnecessary ones into the house. If you are going to drink a quart of bourbon a day or smoke crack, this book is not going to help you. In fact, if you are in the above category, you've probably stolen this book. Give it back. Now.

Problems are the reason human beings are at the top of the food chain. We are the only ones with the brainpower to solve dilemmas. If our ancestors hadn't developed problem-solving skills, they would have vanished like the dinosaurs. In the beginning, before cable, our ancestors the primates lived a marginal existence until a giant animal ate them. That was it. Then we evolved and learned to stick a fiery torch in the giant animal's face. Problem solving separates the successful humans from the ones in the penitentiary. This book is going to help you learn how to solve the inevitable problems that visit every single person on this earth. And don't believe those self-help books that tell you some problems will go away forever. That's a lie. Problems will hunt you down, slap you around, and leave you disillusioned and sometimes broke. That is, unless you meet them at the door and knee them in the groin. Most problems can be neutralized with smarts and sometimes help from others. Your *biggest* advantage will be knowing just who is looking out for you and who is getting a kick out of seeing you suffer. Develop that knowledge, and you're on your way to being a kick-butt problem solver.

But even armed with the knowledge that this book will give you, the struggle to succeed will be intense because you are running uphill against those who have more of everything. But *we* have the numbers. According to Michael Zweig, a professor of economics at the State University of New York at Stony Brook, 62 percent of the labor force in the United States are working-class people. There are many definitions of the working class, but Zweig has come up with a good one: People who do not have much control or authority over the pace or the content of the work and are not the supervisor or the boss. That means you can be a high-priced lawyer billing hours or a sanitation worker cleaning up. If you are not calling your own shots, you are working-class and you need every edge you can get.

This book will get you that edge both in the workplace and at home. We'll analyze the personal part of your existence—your family, friends, teachers, pastor, and so on. These people often have incredible access to your life. They can really help or really hurt you, sometimes without you even knowing about it. And unfortunately, there is no rule that says you are entitled to great parents and relatives and a solid support system. Some lucky Americans get terrific love and guidance from the beginning. Most don't. Instead, many of us have to put up with all kinds of destructive nonsense at home, and much of the time we don't even know what's going on until the damage is done.

But when you finish this book that will all change. You *will* know what's going on.

Who's Looking Out for You? will also deal with external forces that are unleashed against us: the government, the media, the legal system, and others. These powerful entities can crush you unless you understand them and take measures to protect yourself and your family.

Finally, throughout the book I have frankly named the names that need to be named, much as I do on television, on the radio, and in print. Please understand that the examples I provide are based solely on my own instincts. Sometimes I'm wrong about things. And sometimes I even admit it.

But often I'm right because I observe closely and consult widely. Before I blister somebody, I analyze the person carefully, because I do not want to abuse any power I might have. But ultimately, judgments are made in the No Spin Zone. Take this example: I think Bernard Cardinal Law of Boston is a villain. I think he allowed children to be hurt to protect his own reputation in

Rome. Based on the evidence I've seen, Law allowed perverted priests to go unsupervised because he couldn't be bothered with such an inconvenient and potentially embarrassing problem. His main concern, again in my judgment, was holding on to power and avoiding any kind of public scandal that might have tarnished his image with the Pope. The way I see it, Law put his own career above the welfare of little kids. The shepherd of the flock was looking out only for himself.

BUT I COULD BE WRONG!

So while reading this book, please keep that in mind. I will state my case and back it up as best I can. I will lay it all out for you, but, in the end, it is you who must make the final judgment. Only you can determine who is trustworthy and who is not in your life—but you need information and guidelines in order to do that. You need a no-spin road map, pardon the cliché.

And here it comes. However, there is one more point to make before the journey begins. Self-delusions can negate even the best advice and most accurate observations. In order to be truly successful you have to be brutally honest with yourself. Excuses and rationalizations have to be put aside. You must define your own life and not let others do it for you. You must evaluate people and situations the way they *are,* not the way you want them to be. And you must evaluate yourself honestly and absorb the pain that will inevitably cause.

So onward. Let's find out just who is looking out for you.

CHAPTER ONE

Folk Music

Papa don't preach
I'm in trouble deep
But I've made up my mind,
I'm keeping my baby.

—*Madonna, "Papa Don't Preach"*

IT IS BRUTALLY unfair to the children involved, but there are almost 12 million one-parent families in the U.S.A. Single mothers run the majority of those families, and most of those mothers are poor. According to the U.S. census, about 70 percent of all African-American babies are born out of wedlock, as opposed to 27 percent for whites. So do the math and face the result: Millions of American kids are getting hosed from day one.

And there is little any of us can do about it. We live in a free society. If irresponsible people have kids, there is nothing any American authority can do to stop it. In China they kill babies. In some Islamic countries they'll kill a woman who gets pregnant without a husband, or even has sex outside of marriage. These policies, of course, are barbaric and constitute major human rights violations because, believe it or not, women and babies are human beings too.

Here in the good old U.S.A. our Constitution gives careless, foolish citizens all the leeway in the world to bring children into the world and then not care for them. Millions of fathers abandon their kids—and it is rare that any of them sees a day in jail. We all know people who are absolutely awful to their children, just as we all know heroic parents, single and otherwise, who raise successful, happy children despite heavy odds.

There is no question that our society has now embraced the casual approach when it comes to having children. Columnist Kathleen Parker nailed it. "Today having a baby is like swinging through McDonald's for a burger. One baby all the way, hold the dad."

And the damage is incalculable. Over the next two years, about 40 percent of American babies will be born out of wedlock. One million teenagers are likely to have a child this year, and only three in ten will be married. Half of all the mothers who have kids in their teens will be poor *the rest of their lives*. The government spits out these stats like baseball players spit out sunflower seed shells. The politicians use these poor children as pawns in the never-ending game of government entitlements. Society recognizes the problem but can't solve it. Almost all of our social ills can be traced back to chaotic homes.

Luckily, most of us are born into a home with two parents. And thanks to Norman Rockwell and Walt Disney, there is an ideal embedded in many of our minds. Two loving parents, clean clothes, nice toys, a picket fence around the yard, and a dog named Barney.

Does that sound like your household?

My home was a mixture of tradition and chaos. My father wasn't Ozzie Nelson, the TV ideal dad in the '50s and '60s, but he wasn't Ozzy Osbourne either. I wrote about my late father in *The O'Reilly Factor,* the book, and I think it is safe to say that I had a rough-hewn upbringing. Simply put: There was *plenty* of tension in my house. Along with a lot of yelling and martial arts. My father was the Kung and I was the Fu. The perceptive writer James Ellroy, writing in *GQ* magazine, had an interesting take on my upbringing.

[O'Reilly's] old man died of melanoma. He was a rough-edged guy. Fear ran him. He peaked in World War II. He was a naval officer. He did important work in the Jap Occupation. He settled in Levittown, New York. He raised his son and daughter strict. He worked as an accountant. He hated said work. He stuck with it. Fear made him stick. He lived through the Depression. He fed off pix of hobo shantytowns and bean lines. He stayed spartan middle class. He was class bound by fear. He bought the implicit American line. Stick where you are and wish your kids more.

O'Reilly père held his mud. O'Reilly père cracked a bit on his deathbed. He told his son that he never fulfilled his promise. Bill O'Reilly vowed to do it for him.

The old man gave him some tools. His strict legacy served more than hindered. The old man was a moral exemplar. His preachings were sound. He erred only in this rigid enforcement. The old man ruled by fear. O'Reilly hated it as a kid.

O'Reilly gained respect for it years on. The old man emerged as a teacher. He taught by positive and negative example. He was responsible for his own failures. He was complicit in sustaining the American class system.

Ellroy understood my dad's basic résumé but left out one important item: Despite his ordinary life he was an extremely perceptive man. My father was Abe Lincoln: honest and also knew instinctively who could be trusted and who was auditioning for the role of Judas. But this knowledge did him little good because he was afraid to act on it.

The upside in my house was this: There were standards. There was no binge drinking, no drugs, no cursing, no weird displays of inexplicable behavior (except by me). My folks were like their folks before them—reactors. If I acted like a jerk, the reaction was Allen Iverson quick. My parents did not spare the rod, they brooked no disrespect, and they had no concerns at all about my "self-esteem."

There were times when I hated my father. I admit it. He knew it. The punishment that descended upon me was mostly uncalled-for and born of the frustration of his life. But even in my teens I realized that my parents wanted me to do well and succeed. As dim as I was, I knew that there was love in the house.

S‍o **NOW WHEN** I see children at risk, it makes me furious. Take four-year-old Rilya Wilson, for example. I told her story on *The*

Factor and it is heartbreaking. She was born in East Cleveland, Ohio, and her father split soon after her birth. Her mother was a drug addict and lost parental rights. So little Rilya went to live with her "godmother," Geralyn Graham, in south Florida, a situation that was paid for and supposedly supervised by the state of Florida.

Trouble is, the caseworker assigned to Rilya, Deborah Muskelly, did not make the state-ordered mandatory visits, although, in the state files, she falsely recorded that she had. When Rilya turned up missing from her "home" in early 2001, nobody seemed to care. It took sixteen months for the state of Florida even to find out about it.

Now, you would think the authorities would be all over the case once the facts came to light. A defenseless four-year-old missing and possibly murdered! You would think everyone in power would rally to see justice done.

On television I asked Florida Governor Jeb Bush to get directly involved in the case. He would not. I asked for the resignation of the head of the children's services department. She stayed on for almost a year until the pressure finally forced Bush to sack her. I asked for the caseworker, Muskelly, to be immediately arrested. She was not, and neither Bush nor anyone else offered an explanation. To say the situation was disgraceful is insult-light.

Finally, just before the election of 2002, Governor Bush had to act because he was slipping big in the polls. Both the caseworker and the "godmother" were finally charged. But the hard truth is that nobody in the world cared for little Rilya Wilson. Nobody looked out for her even though a number of adults were being paid to do that. And so she's still missing and most likely dead. Next time you have parental issues, think about Rilya.

Poverty is an enormous problem for children, but even having money often doesn't solve the parental dilemma. Let's take a look at Julio and Enrique Iglesias, the father and son singers. These guys are fabulously wealthy, so it is hard to believe that with all their talent and fame, a smooth relationship did not evolve. But according to *Parade* magazine, the two are now rivals in the world of pop music. Enrique Iglesias is quoted as saying this about his famous father: "It's not a normal relationship. After I sold millions of records he [Julio] would say 'but you'll never win a Grammy.'"

Nice. Julio Iglesias has been blessed with enormous material success but apparently is competing with his own son for outside adulation. Does that make sense? Of course not. As everybody knows, money and privilege can screw a kid up fast. Enrique Iglesias was the product of a very messy divorce. As a young child, he lived with his mother in Spain. But her journalism career caused him to be left often in the care of a nanny. When Enrique turned seven, he was sent to live with his father in Miami. But according to friends, the child had to learn music outside this house because he was afraid Julio would put him down. Enrique has become a music superstar, but his road was tougher than some might think.

In a perfect world, every parent would love, nurture, and protect his or her children. If anyone should be looking out for you, it is your mother and father. But as we know, there are no parental guarantees in this life. You can ask Enrique Iglesias, or, if you get to heaven, you can ask Rilya Wilson.

Many of us are deeply conflicted about our parents. My father and mother certainly provided for me and made damn sure I got educated and was taught the essentials of life. But can I say that my father was always looking out for me? No, I can't. My mother's instincts were much more in that direction, but my father had demons that intruded on his parental duties. As with millions of other American parents, my father set a terrible example by inflicting unnecessary pain on his children. He did not do this on purpose. He simply could not control himself.

And therein lies the big parental dilemma. Just like everyone else, a parent might have to do battle with a powerful inner demon—that part of the mental makeup that is self-destructive and evil. If those demons win the battle, the child as well as the parent takes the hit. Abandonment, abuse, addiction, and apathy can scar a child for life. And there's little the kid can do about it.

Ask psychiatrists and they will tell you that children who are mentally or physically abused often grow up to be abusers themselves. In the ongoing scandal in the Roman Catholic priesthood, for example, it's become clear that many of the abusers were themselves abused when they were young.

This is not an excuse, but it may be a partial explanation. And once understood, the cycle of emotional or physical abuse that spins down from one generation to the next has a better chance of being stopped. It takes awareness. It takes courage. It takes discipline.

Most of us have unresolved problems with our parents. Some of these problems are trivial, some much more intense. For your own welfare it is important that you get to the root of the parental issue and ask this question: Did your parents really look out for you? Did they want you to have a happy and successful life? The question is a bear, frightening and unpredictable. It can be painful even thinking about it. But here are a few guidelines to clear the air a little.

Call them the Ten Commandments of Effective Parenting.

1. A parent who is looking out for you will make time for you if he or she possibly can. Hint: Serial golfing is no excuse.
2. All punishments will fit the crime. Discipline is essential, but no parent should inflict frequent physical or mental pain on a kid. Childhood is supposed to be a wondrous, joyful period. Parents are the grown-ups and have to be patient, within reason. Words can deeply wound a child. Parents must display kindness and understanding. Corporal punishment should be a last resort, and used within guidelines that have been clearly established before any physical punishment is administered.
3. Parents who are looking out for their children will be under control in the house. There will be no random violence, intoxication, sexual displays, uncontrolled anger, or vile language (sorry, Ozzy). The house should be a refuge, a place where the child feels protected and loved. If it is a chaotic mess, the parents are not looking out for the kids.
4. If a parent is looking out for the child, he or she will educate that child in the best possible way. That includes paying college tuition if at all possible. Parents owe it to the kids to give them the tools to compete, and those tools are often expensive. But they come before the vacation, the Harley, the leaf

blower. If you don't want to sacrifice for your children, don't have them.

5. Parents should be available at all times for emergency talks. "All access," as the rock stars say. No excuses here. Ditch the meeting, get back from the mall, get off the phone. There is nothing more important than dealing with a child's crisis immediately, even if it seems trivial to the parent.

6. If a parent is looking out for the child, then that child's friends will be screened, the kid's whereabouts will be known at all times, and scholastic progress will be monitored daily. Homework will be looked at and questions about school will be asked. That's how trouble is spotted before it gets out of hand; that's how you bring out the best in your child. Children know you have a strong interest in their lives. They may bitch, but kids badly want that kind of attention. All the research shows that close parental monitoring is the leading factor in whether or not adolescents will engage in high-risk behavior.

7. Rules will be enforced but explained. Parents who truly look out for their kids understand that there are rules in society and that high standards of behavior are the key to a successful life. Rules are good. But rules must have a logical objective. "Because I say so" can be effective when the kid gets stubborn, but before that conversation stopper is trotted out, try connecting some dots with your child. It doesn't always work, but the effort is worth it.

8. Parents will be honest at all times. Lead by example. No lying, no cheating, no nasty gossip, no cruelty, no manipulating, no jealousy toward your kids, no competing with them, no

overindulging their various whims, and no overprotecting. Parents who are looking out for their children will prepare them for the rigors of this world. They will educate them *after* school, encourage generosity and spirituality, and generally do the right thing *all the time*. Or at least in front of them.

9. Parents will be respectful of *their* parents. Grandparent abuse or neglect is among the worst possible things a child can see. This is a very important commandment. You can't effectively look out for your kids if you don't look out for your folks. (Even if your folks don't deserve it.)

10. Finally, effective parents will remove the TVs and computers from their kids' rooms. All media absorption should be done in public space. This is a dangerous world, and the danger is now in the house. If a parent is really looking out for the kid, subversive material must be kept to an absolute minimum. Corrupting influences on children are everywhere, and parents must be full-time firefighters. Life is tough and getting tougher. The demons, the exploiters, want your kids. You must look out for them. Fight hard.

So, did your parents obey all the commandments? Chances are they did not—they are human, after all, even though few kids take that into consideration. The key question once you reach adulthood is, did your folks *try* to do the right thing by you? If they did make an effort, then they were looking out for you. If they didn't, then they were not. End of story?

Well, not quite. If you truly believe that your parents failed you, what then? It seems to me that you have a couple of choices. You can resent them for the rest of your life, which is a colossal waste of time and energy. Or you can do NOTHING. That's right, nada. You can't change anything, so drop it. This is a HUGE lesson. Everybody has bad stuff happen to him or her in life. Sometimes your parents are the bad stuff. Let it go.

HERE'S A PERSONAL STORY. In the 2002 NBA finals some idiot gave Shaquille O'Neal's father courtside seats at the home court of the New Jersey Nets. The powerful L.A. Laker knew his father was there but would not look at him. That's because the guy, I won't call him a man, walked away from Shaq when he was a baby and never returned.

I say, good for O'Neal. By all accounts his mother is a very special woman and Shaq is devoted to her. He has obviously succeeded in the NBA, and right now he is a positive influence in this country. He has a right to ignore a father who did not look out for him.

And for good measure I hope the deadbeat dad knows how much O'Neal is making putting balls through hoops. How about close to $30 million a year!

Most parent-child relationships are not as clear-cut as Shaquille O'Neal's. Many of us have very conflicted emotions about our parents; it is hard to nail down the absolute truth. But you definitely have to sort it out and decide the best course of action.

Here's what I did. When I was seventeen my father and I had a mini-brawl. Lamps were broken; my mother was horrified. But it had to happen. The man had to learn that no longer would his son put up with his unreasonable wrath. And my father surrendered. He knew the physical stuff had to stop. His words were exactly these: "You're on your own."

Fine. I went away to college and began to compete. It wasn't easy, but I made my way. I spent summers living at home but moved out entirely after graduation. But I always kept in touch and I was always respectful. Eventually, any resentment I had stored up dissipated because I understood that to harbor it would hurt the entire family. So as Hyman Roth told Michael Corleone while discussing the dueling atrocities of their two gangs, "I let it go."

But I also did a lot of serious thinking about my father's behavior and how it compared with the role of a parent who is really looking out for his child. I think it is worth restating the theme of the commandments: *The primary duty of a parent is to give his or her children the tools to build a happy and successful life. These tools are educational, emotional, and spiritual.* If your parents or parent did this, that person truly was looking out for you. And you are one lucky stiff.

CHAPTER TWO

It's My Party

It's my party
And I'll cry if I want to.

—*Lesley Gore, "It's My Party"*

SO, WHO THE heck are you anyway? Are you looking out only for yourself, for Numero Uno? This may surprise you, but if you are a poster child for the Me Generation, you are in dire trouble.

Here's the "no-spin" truth: America and France lead the world in self-absorption. The U.S.A. is the most powerful country the world has ever seen, but our culture has been polluted by the "where's mine" theme. We see it everywhere, in constant media advertising about possessions and good times and products to make us look as buff and alluring as possible. From the time they are conscious of the outside world, American babies are bombarded with messages of consumption in a way that brainwashes them, sometimes permanently. The buying power of the American consumer drives the country and is as addictive as nicotine. Wall Street depends on it, and the government protects it. The human brain is not fully formed until age twenty-five, but by age three the American brain is already screaming, "I want *stuff*."

Up until about forty years ago, most Americans didn't have enough money to get hooked on consumption. Credit cards were nonexistent; you had to pay as you went. But the sixties changed everything. All of a sudden it was "Do your own thing" and "If it feels good, do it." You don't have enough dough? Here's a line of credit to make it all happen. Before you could say boo, the baby boomers took off on a gold rush of acquisition and an intense quest for self-satisfaction. At first the '60s movement was driven by social consciousness, but greedy boomers rushing to embrace the philosophy of abundance soon overran the passive hippies.

One problem with the comfort addiction is that it takes a lot of money, energy, and thought to feed the habit. And all of that thought is *about you*. In the '80s, Hall and Oates wrote a song called "Possession Obsession." The refrain says it all:

> *Don't you know it's a matter of fact,*
> *The more that you take, the less you give back.*

But so what, you say. So freakin' what? What's wrong with taking care of Number One? Well, listen up: If you're always thinking about yourself, you'll rarely look out for anyone else. And you'll soon run out of people who will *look out for you*. Why's that? Well, let me break this to you gently: *Generous people will not associate with self-ish jerks.* It simply will not happen. To have a friend, you have to *be* a friend. That's an old Irish saying, and at times the Irish do know what they are talking about. Just don't get them at closing time.

Convinced?

No? Okay, time then to bust another myth, the one about "bad companions." You know, the people your parents told you to stay away from. Well, you don't have to stay away from them because if you're a decent person, *they'll stay away from you*. Nobody doing bad things wants you around if you are not in sync with their destructive agenda. Walk into any bar and order a Dr Pepper, the booze hounds will mock you. You're not welcome at a methamphetamine party if you won't indulge, and you're not wanted at an Enron executive meeting if you're not willing to rob other people blind.

The corrupt seek out each other, so if you are hanging around with Tony Soprano, you are *already* a degenerate. Tony would never have let you into the Bada Bing in the first place if you weren't.

It's important for all Americans to recognize that only good people can really look out for you. Bad people are looking out for themselves and will use you. They will pretend to have your best interests at heart but will kick you in the head when your usefulness to them expires. But a good friend will last a lifetime. And that person will look out for you if you demonstrate you are worth looking out for.

So my premise is simple—before you can find help in this world, you have to develop qualities that are respected by good people. If you are selfish, shallow, money-grubbing, manipulative, callous, violent, petty, envious, gossipy, or self-destructive, then you will soon be on your own. Nobody will ever look out for you with the possible exception of your mom. She is compelled by nature to do so.

Now, all of us occasionally do bad things and act selfishly, but self-interest must not define us. I use the term "weasel" a lot when talking about untrustworthy people. Weasels are by nature small carnivores that hunt alone at night, in the dark, and viciously kill their weaker prey. There are legions of human weasels in America today. They have dens where they hang out with other weasels. But if you are not one of them, they don't want you in the den. And believe me, you don't want to be there, because if there is just one morsel of weasel food, it will not be shared. The strongest weasel will take it, and the other weasels will starve. There are no socialist weasels.

It is amazing to me that many of us just cannot tell the good people from the bad people these days. In my adulthood I have seen a lot of marriages break up, and I'm always amazed that the aggrieved party didn't see it coming. Selfish, manipulative people usually are not subtle. Their character is obvious to any perceptive person. The problem is that most Americans do not see people for what they really are—they see them for what *they want them to be*. Remember the self-delusion factor I mentioned in the introduction.

How many times have you seen friends or family attach themselves to just the worst person this side of Saddam Hussein? Everybody knows the person is pond scum except your friend. And then when the bad person finally turns on your friend, he or she is stunned, betrayed, bewildered. Psychoanalysts make a fortune treating such naive people.

But here's some free advice (well, not exactly—you did buy the book): Watch how your new friend or lover treats people other than you. Watch how she treats her parents. If he's divorced, find out why. If she's dysfunctional, run like hell even if she does look like Heidi Klum. Adults rarely change unless desperately motivated to do so. No matter how good, kind, generous, and loving *you* are, the heavy odds are that an emotionally damaged person will remain damaged and a bad person will remain bad *no matter what you do*. So screw it, you are not supposed to be St. Paul. Conversions of any kind are tough and nearly impossible to achieve if you become emotionally involved. Walk briskly away from destructive people and find generous people to hang out with. Then you'll have a chance of finding an effective support system in life.

M<small>Y</small> **FATHER TRUSTED** almost no one. Thus, he had no one looking out for him except my mother, and her power was, shall we say, limited. It's not that my father was a bad guy—he wasn't. He despised bad guys. He would glare at them and dismissively call them "Chief." They got the message and didn't mess with him.

But my dad also did not cultivate good people because he was a suspicious guy. The few friends he had were working stiffs who retreated from the world just as he did. William O'Reilly, Sr., worked in a company for thirty-five years and nobody with any pull ever looked out for him. He closed himself off from the two-way street that is loyalty.

My grandfather didn't have a support system either, because he was even more suspicious than my father, which put him in the same category as Ebenezer Scrooge. John O'Reilly was a New York City cop who worked the waterfront during Prohibition. He was one tough SOB. But when he left the department he pretty much retired from life. He stayed out of the fray, rarely offering advice or support, and let my father fend for himself.

Unfortunately, he didn't know how. He had great talent. He was witty, quick-thinking, honest, and well-spoken. But nobody gave him direction. So as James Ellroy pointed out, my dad "held his mud." If somebody had been looking out for William O'Reilly, Sr., his life might have been very different. But my father never sought out good people who might have helped him. And so he didn't find any. You can go only so far solo in this world. My father did not get very far, and on his deathbed he told me his biggest regret was that he never lived up to his potential.

LIFE IS MOST definitely your party, and as Lesley Gore sang in the semi-innocent early '60s, "You can cry if you want to." Lots of folks spend their lives doing just that. But your pursuit of happiness will not be advanced by self-pity. It will not be advanced by fear and poor judgment. What will help you greatly in life is the wisdom and caring of good people. If you are going to devote so much time to shopping, go shopping for *them*. Oh, and one more thing: Cultivating and nurturing good friends is not easy. Every two years I put together a trip for a bunch of my male friends from all over the world. Some people are amazed that I can get a couple of dozen guys to show up in a place like Hawaii for a few laughs and a little hell-raising. But these are people who know the value of friendship. I have spent a lifetime assembling these friends, and I know they look out for me just as I look out for them. A few years ago eighteen of us met in the Virgin Islands and an editor for the magazine *Cigar Aficionado*, Terry Fagin, tagged along. Here are some of his observations:

> What brought this group together was friendship with Bill O'Reilly, the executive producer and anchor of *The O'Reilly Factor*. All of these men had crossed paths with O'Reilly at some point in their lives, some as early as a shared childhood in Levittown, Long Island, during the Eisenhower administration.
>
> "I go back with O'Reilly to first grade," says John Blasi. "The vacations are a natural extension of our childhood routine. I would come home from school and call O'Reilly to see what game he had pulled together and where we were to meet."
>
> Anyone who watches O'Reilly's talk show can glean a few basic traits about the man. He's smart, quick, opinionated, and doesn't suffer fools gladly. "I've known O'Reilly for twenty-nine years. Success hasn't changed him. He's as much a pain in the ass today as he was back then," jokes Mike Dutko, a cop turned defense lawyer from Florida. "But he's brutally frank and fiercely loyal. He expects nothing less from his friends. He also believes that friendship requires effort and commitment." It's a loyalty that his friends return.

So why have I bothered tracking these guys throughout my life? What's in it for me? Well, the answer is nothing much in worldly terms. I've been very lucky and never had to ask anyone for anything substantial. But the men—and some women in different circumstances—I deal with as friends all have attributes that I admire. They all are honest, so I can get perspective and no-spin opinion on any subject. And if I ever am in dire need—say, I lost my job or became very ill—I know these guys would help me in any way they could. Finally, if you follow me on television and radio, you know I often have to walk an editorial tightrope, taking tough positions and sometimes hammering very powerful people. It helps to have people I trust there to tell me if I go too far or even not far enough. Not that I always follow the advice, but I do listen.

So how many people do you have looking out for you? Or a better question might be, how many nonfamily members are you looking out for? The second query is the crux of the matter. If you can't tick off five people who would bleed for you, there's a problem. Remember, this "looking-out-for" stuff takes time and energy. It takes smarts and reflection. But it is a key to having the best possible life.

And it doesn't matter who you are. If you cannot convince quality people to look out for you, you are in trouble. Consider the beautiful singer Mariah Carey, who has money, fame, and power. Here's what she told *Vibe* magazine after her emotional meltdown: "No one was looking out for the human being that existed inside the machine that pays everybody." Ms. Carey learned the hard way.

THE RICH AND POWERFUL have an advantage that everyday people do not have. Here's an example: In September 2002, I was invited to attend the annual Forstmann-Little get-together in

Aspen, Colorado. Teddy Forstmann is a philanthropist business-man who puts together a weekend full of panels and discussions featuring some of America's most successful citizens. I usually don't attend events like this because I don't feel comfortable among the swells. But Forstmann does some good things with his dough. He wanted me to talk about heroism, so I said okay and saddled up for the Rockies.

The crowd was big-name city: Rudy Giuliani, Martha Stewart, Tom Brokaw, Diane Sawyer, Roger Staubach, Prince Andrew, Lance Armstrong, Senator John Glenn, Queen Noor, Alan Greenspan, Karl Rove, Charlie Rose, and on and on. Corporate titans were wandering around all over the place. It was a giant flea market of power, with the focus on networking and information. These kinds of weekends forge alliances and lead to social and business contacts—sometimes even to friendships. They are part of the privileged game that powerful Americans enjoy. Access to those at the top is limited, but if you have it, many good things can happen for you.

I tried my best to be pleasant. Not an easy thing for your hum-ble correspondent because I am awful at small talk and trivial pur-suits. The truth is that I did manage to tee off Queen Noor, the widow of Jordan's King Hussein. I believe she thought I was a complete barbarian when I told the group that the reason the Arab world would never give the United States a break was that we support Israel and many Arabs hate the Jews. Upon hearing that, the queen turned a couple of different colors, but it's the truth, so I had no sympathy for her.

After offending the queen, I went on to say that anyone could perform a heroic act, but that doesn't make one a hero. In order to be a true hero, you have to be a person of honesty and strong character. Someone who puts others ahead of himself. I am not quite sure how the crowd digested that one, but they were well-mannered and no dinner rolls were heaved in my direction.

In the two days I spent with those affluent people I learned plenty. I always knew the powerful protected one another, but now I know they enjoy one another's company as well. High up there in the mountains of Colorado was a lesson that every person should be exposed to: Life is a lot easier if you have folks looking out for you, and if they happen to be powerful, that is not a bad thing. Just don't sell your soul for access.

But the sad truth is that most of us will never have the aristocracy on our team. I certainly didn't, and now I don't really care about the powerful other than keeping an eye on them. But that doesn't diminish the point: You need other people to help you fulfill your potential. And if you're lucky enough to have Bill Gates thinking that you're swell, the up escalator can kick into gear real fast.

FINALLY, WHATEVER HAPPENS at my life party, I have chosen not to cry—at least in public. But I have privately lamented friends lost through acts of God, and also some of those who have betrayed me. In my younger days my selection process of people to trust was badly flawed. In short, I rushed things. I confided in people I had known only a brief time and was badly burned on a number of occasions. Because I had grown up in a tight-knit neighborhood where deception was rare, I foolishly thought the business world would contain comrades like my friends back home.

Did I hear somebody say the word "naive"? Actually, I was far beyond naive, I was just plain dumb, and I'll describe some of my major miscalculations later in this book. I believe you'll be amused.

But once somebody betrayed my trust, that somebody rarely got a second chance. I was done with that person unless I received a full explanation and some contrition.

One quick example before we get to the American government chapter, which features loads of betrayal. Years ago I was friends with a fellow broadcaster. Because we were both single and liked the ladies, we had some great times. In most social situations I make it a policy to let everybody know what the cost of the event or evening would likely be. And I am always rigidly fair because I have a solid rule: Never scam your friends.

Anyway, on a trip to Colorado for a little rest and relaxation, I told the guy how much he owed for the hotel room that he and I were splitting. He paused, and then asked to see the bill. Okay, fine, I showed him the bill. Then he questioned why he should pay half of the parking charge. Well, since I had paid the entire car rental fee—and he was riding around in that car—I had assumed the car parking fee would be split.

But that wasn't the point. I waved the discussion to a close and picked up the parking. It was chump change, not worth the discussion. But that was it for the guy. Number one, he didn't trust me on the bill, even though I had never shortchanged him in the fifteen years we had known each other. Indeed, he often benefited financially in our travels because of discounts I got from my job and frequent-flyer miles, things like that. And number two, the entire matter was not about money—it was about power. For some reason unbeknownst to me, the guy was asserting himself.

Now, some people might have argued, tried to understand, or even become bitter. Not me. I just walked away. If the guy had later apologized, I might have dealt with him again. But he did not. And since a person who doesn't trust you cannot possibly look out for you or even be a friend, there was no further common ground on which that man and I could stand. He was history.

In the end, you are not what you eat. Rather, you *are* whom you associate with. If you run around with despicable people, the heavy odds are that you are despicable as well. And if you are paying somebody for advice—beware. Many "therapists" are looking out for your checkbook, not you. So let's dispense with the psychobabble and set up a simple rule to live by: People who give you intoxicants, an unnecessary hard time, dishonest answers, or anything consistently destructive are to be rejected. Any wavering in this regard and you are taking the entrance ramp onto the sad-life highway.

For when it is all over and you are leaving this life, the difference between my father's death and yours will be the people you let into your life. If you embrace honest, caring, and strong people, I can almost guarantee that you will have accomplished many positive things on this earth. But if you go it alone or book passage on the ship of fools, expect one of those fools to toss you over the side when the big waves come. And if you *still* don't believe me, then listen to George Washington, the father of the greatest country the world has ever seen. George is my go-to guy on "looking out for you" quotes: "Associate yourself with men of quality if you esteem your own reputation, for 'tis better to be alone than in bad company."

You tell them, G.W. Bad company will never look out for you.

CHAPTER THREE

My Country
'Tis of Thee

Keep on rockin' in the free world.

—*Neil Young, "Rockin' in the Free World"*

NO QUESTION ABOUT it, the U.S.A. is a great place to live if you are willing to get an education, work hard, and persist in the pursuit of happiness. There is, however, one important and somewhat disturbing question: Are the powers that be in America looking out for you?

The answer is very clear: no, not really.

Surprised? You shouldn't be. America was built on self-reliance and ruthless demands on the individual. Among the Founding Fathers and subsequent presidents and leaders were few who would attend a pity party. James Garfield, our twentieth president, was once asked on the campaign trail about poverty in America. Said Jim: "Poverty is uncomfortable, I can testify, but nine times out of ten the best thing that can happen to a young man is to be tossed overboard and compelled to sink or swim for himself."

Sink?

And our twenty-sixth president, Teddy Roosevelt, was even blunter: "Pray not for lighter burdens, but for stronger backs."

Strength?

Until the mid-1930s, America was a nation that basically said to its citizens: "Your forefathers have given you freedom, so good luck, see you around, hope you make it." Then came the Great Depression, World War II, the Great Society, the Age of Aquarius, the Me Generation, and finally the anything-goes Clinton years. Throughout those generations everything changed. While John Kennedy once asked what you would do for your country, modern politicians were suddenly lining up to tell you what they were going to give you, and one of the biggest entitlement pushers around was JFK's brother, Senator Edward Kennedy. Most give-away programs have been complete failures, but the rhetorical battle continues to this day.

The harsh truth is this: Those running the federal government make a lot of promises but deliver very little, because the system is designed not to aid the individual. In the year 2001, the federal government spent nearly two trillion dollars. Who the hell can keep track of that much money? The answer is nobody. As I pointed out in my last book, *The No Spin Zone,* no government agency even watches how the tax dollars are spent! So money is stolen or wasted, and programs turn into chaos with a depressing regularity. It is only when disaster strikes that Congress calls in the General Accounting Office for an investigative audit.

Let's be realistic here. The country simply cannot look out for you because a) there are almost 300 million "yous" in the U.S.A., and b) it basically doesn't want to.

Sure, you'll get an inflation-eaten Social Security check when you hit sixty-five, and, if you wash out, you might get some unemployment insurance or welfare or other "assistance." But this is chump change, designed only to keep you from living beneath a bridge someplace. The truth is that the country wants you to get a good job so that you can buy stuff and pay a lot of taxes. But the country is not going to help you get that job. It will, however, help itself to about half your paycheck if you do manage to prosper.

And once the government takes your money, it will not watch where it is spent. Tax dollars are a major tool that politicians use to buy votes. But once the voting is done, they are not real interested in tracking expenditures. The best example of this is the "Big Dig" construction scandal in Massachusetts, perhaps the biggest taxpayer rip-off in the history of the United States. The following is hard to believe, but it is the gospel truth.

In 1987, President Reagan vetoed the Surface Transportation and Uniform Relocation Assistance Act. Senators Edward Kennedy and Robert Byrd of West Virginia then threatened to pull a number of agricultural subsidies unless senators like North Carolina's Terry Sanford supported the bill and kept it alive in the Senate. Sanford caved and the bill was passed after Mr. Reagan left office and signed by President Bush the elder. Kennedy was thrilled when $2.5 billion federal was approved for the "Big Dig," which was going to modernize highways and tunnels in the South End of Boston. Later Kennedy got an additional $100 million more thrown into the pot.

Initially budgeted by Massachusetts authorities at $2.6 billion, the "Dig" has now cost us American taxpayers close to $15 billion, and money is still being spent. For ten years, Senators Kennedy and John Kerry, and Governors Weld, Celluci, and Swift all looked the other way as tax money was looted by organized crime, corrupt unions, and incompetent management on the vast construction project. Nobody in power gave a damn or intervened in any effective way, because money was pouring into Boston and the geese were getting fat. This kind of stuff happens all the time in America, albeit not on the same massive scale as the "Big Dig."

If you call Ted Kennedy's office and ask him for a comment on the "Big Dig," he will blow you off. His hometown newspaper, the *Boston Globe*, did a year-long investigation on the "Dig" that documented massive fraud and corruption. Kennedy would not talk to them.

SO WISE UP and accept the no-spin reality: Our federal government is not good at helping real people who have real problems, and it doesn't care about the money you give it as long as that revenue train keeps chugging along. But don't despair entirely. Here are some of the things the federal government *is* good at:

- Waging war
- Collecting taxes from individuals (not corporations)
- Talking about the future of "our kids"

- Talking about the future of the frozen tundra
- Letting Jesse Jackson get away with using his nonprofit organizations for his own enrichment
- Sending Congresspeople on lavish "fact-finding" trips to the far corners of the earth (First Lady Hillary Clinton was the poster lady for this)
- Keeping Camp David looking spiffy
- Keeping corruption investigations of powerful elected officials secret
- Not really trying to find out anything relevant during those multimillion-dollar investigations
- Incarcerating suspected terrorists without charging or trying them (not that that is a bad thing if you find some guy from Yemen in the mountains of Afghanistan armed with grenades and wearing an "I love Osama" T-shirt)

And here are some of the things the federal government is *not* good at:

- Locating guys named Osama Bin Laden and Mullah Omar (I hope by the time this book is published that the CIA has at least a clue)
- Stopping illegal aliens from entering the country
- Investigating rich and powerful guys who make secret deals, like Marc Rich and Bill Clinton
- Investigating a guy named Senator Robert Torricelli, who took gifts from a Korean guy named David Chang

- Investigating a town in New York that voted 1,400 to 12 for Hillary Clinton after she visited said town during her 2000 senatorial campaign; a few months after her election, her husband, the President, issued pardons for some town big shots who were serving time for massive fraud
- Investigating guys named Roger Clinton and Hugh Rodham, who apparently received lots of money for doing nothing but mentioning possible presidential pardons to a variety of bad guys
- Running a taxpayer-funded railroad named Amtrak that has lost almost $100 billion (that's right, Dr. Evil, $100 *billion*)
- Building highways, bridges, and tunnels that don't involve billions of dollars in cost overruns
- Keeping the Mafia out of those construction projects
- Figuring out that not imposing gas mileage standards hurts every single American except those making and driving SUVs (by the way, our failure to conserve oil put $10 billion a year into Saddam Hussein's bloody pocket)

If you analyze these lists closely, you'll find a common thread: You get screwed while powerful, corrupt people skate. Does that sound like the feds are looking out for you?

HERE'S HOW BAD it really is. Corruption, incompetence, and political correctness have spread like the Ebola virus throughout our federal system, and the lack of a disciplined approach to controlling our enemies and securing our borders is one of the main reasons that three thousand Americans were murdered on September 11, 2001. To understand what has happened we have to go back to 1996 and peek into an Oval Office meeting between the aforementioned President Clinton and Senator Torricelli.

Called "The Torch" because of his volcanic temper, New Jersey's former senator deftly cultivated a neoliberal political persona that mixed pragmatism with pandering. Because New Jersey is home to hundreds of thousands of newly arrived Hispanic immigrants, Torricelli played to the home team and became deeply involved with a variety of issues that struck emotional chords with the new citizens.

In 1995, a Guatemalan colonel named Julio Roberto Alpirez was linked to the murder of an American in that chaotic country. For decades the Guatemalan army had been systemically assassinating leftist rebel leaders and those who they thought supported them. Alpirez apparently controlled some of those death squads even as he was on the CIA payroll as an informer, a situation not uncommon the world over. Throughout the Cold War, the Central Intelligence Agency often paid rightist thugs for information that could be used against Communist agitators. The CIA calls these informants "assets."

Anyway, Torricelli, then a congressman, went public with the story, embarrassed the CIA, and enlisted President Clinton to "reform" the informer payroll. Sensing political gain, Mr. Clinton ordered the CIA to stop paying any informer suspected of human rights violations or who had a felony conviction on his record. Any exceptions had to be approved by the CIA brass in Langley, Virginia. President Clinton's order became known as "the Torricelli Principle."

Within months, U.S. ground intelligence virtually dried up. Scores of CIA station chiefs submitted their retirement papers, knowing they could not gather intelligence as effectively as they had during the Cold War. Without the criminal element informing on the criminal element, the CIA became deaf. Bad people know what other bad people are doing. Mother Teresa does not.

These grizzled veterans who retired from the Agency were often replaced by young officers with little or no field experience and no contacts in the shadowy world of counterintelligence. Thus Osama Bin Laden and his murderous zealots developed Al Qaeda with little scrutiny from the CIA. By presidential mandate the U.S. national security apparatus could not associate with terrorists who might have infiltrated the group or even pay for information about it. Al Qaeda managed to bomb two U.S. embassies and the USS *Cole* with few problems because our federal government had minimal intelligence on the missions.

Incredibly, even after those attacks, the Torricelli Principle remained in place. It was only after the catastrophe on September 11 that President Bush ordered it out of existence.

THE FBI ENDURED a similar situation under President Clinton. Because Mr. Clinton and then FBI chief Louis Freeh despised each other, little information was shared between the Bureau and the Executive Branch. Early in the Clinton administration, Director Freeh was deeply embarrassed that FBI files found their way into the hands of the Clintons at the White House. Some believe those files were copied and later used for political purposes.

Even worse, Freeh knew that Attorney General Janet Reno was blocking all the campaign-finance-related investigations involving the President and Vice President, and all evidence that Mr. Clinton and Al Gore were lying to the American people was being systematically buried by the Justice Department. The bitterness between Freeh and Clinton is documented in the book *Age of Sacred Terror,* written by two counterterrorism experts who worked for Clinton's national security team. They accurately report that Freeh simply would not tell the White House anything relevant about specific terrorism intelligence that the bureau had developed. The result was that Mr. Clinton and his security advisers were shut out of information about terrorism domestically by Freeh and internationally by the insane Torricelli Principle. And many of us wondered how September 11 could have happened?

But, astonishingly, innocent Americans dead in the streets were not enough for the federal government to change its ways and actually begin protecting its citizens. Faced with as many as 10 million illegal aliens freely moving about the U.S.A., the Bush administration inexplicably stood by and did very little to stem the tide of illegal immigration. The President would not order the military to the border areas to back up the Border Patrol, and millions of illegals continued to stream across from Mexico and Canada into the U.S.A. An interesting side note: President Bush did ask Canadian Prime Minister Jean Chrétien to tighten up Canada's immigration policies, which allow entry to pretty much anyone who shows up. Canada also provides generous welfare payments to most immigrants without doing many background checks. The Right Honorable Chrétien, through a translator, diplomatically told the American President to get, well, bent. A few months later Chrétien's foreign minister called President Bush "stupid."

But even as Mr. Bush was putting pressure on our friends to the north to control illegal aliens, he was allowing former Paine-Webber executive James Ziglar to run the Immigration and Naturalization Service, one of the most inept agencies in our nation's history. By most accounts, Commissioner Ziglar was completely clueless. On his watch, INS policies continued to be disorganized and sometimes downright dangerous. The Census Bureau actually gave up counting the illegals because the numbers became so great. Three of the 9/11 hijackers were in the U.S.A. illegally.

AND BECAUSE James Ziglar and the INS did not learn from the Al Qaeda attack, history was to repeat itself in the sensational sniper murder case. In October 2002, the press learned that seventeen-year-old Lee Boyd Malvo, aka John Lee Malvo, who together with forty-one-year-old John Allen Muhammad shot at least fifteen Americans, killing ten of them, had actually been released without supervision from the custody of the INS. Malvo, a Jamaican national, was apprehended by the Border Patrol along with his mother, Una James, near Seattle in January 2002. The

Border Patrol classified the pair as stowaways, handing them over to the INS with an "immediate deportation" recommendation. But the INS overruled the Border Patrol and released Malvo and his mother into the wind. Here's the background to this sorry episode:

Malvo and his mother had been smuggled into the United States aboard a ship late in the year 2000. Subsequently, James got a job at a Red Lobster on the Gulf Coast near Naples, Florida. But the teenager migrated northwest to Washington State to join up with John Muhammad, an unemployed drifter who apparently had met Malvo and his mother earlier on the island of Antigua, a common transit point for illegals coming by ship to the United States.

By December 2001 Una James had also moved to Washington State. There she asked police to find her son, who she suspected was under the influence of Muhammad. Soon after the cops picked up Malvo, detectives realized both son and mother were illegal aliens. They were turned over to the Border Patrol, where agents did the paperwork and expected to see the pair deported.

But Seattle INS official Blake Brown did not want to deport Malvo and his mother. He ordered the Border Patrol to change the pair's status so they could stay in the U.S.A. pending an immigration hearing. The Border Patrol refused. So Brown took unilateral action and changed the designation himself, possibly violating the Immigration Reform Act. Malvo and his mother were released; the rest is history. The teenager has confessed to more than a dozen murders. So what explains the strange actions of the INS? Hold on, you're about to get angry.

As soon as I began to investigate the Malvo case on *The O'Reilly*

Factor, I quickly found out why Brown did not want to issue a deportation order. It was the expense. Yes, you read that right. Even after 9/11, many INS officials are under pressure from Washington to keep the deportations of illegal aliens to a minimum because they are expensive. In this case, however, the Border Patrol was so furious that Malvo and his mother were set free, it broke Brown's cover and fed *The Factor* primary-source information.

We took that information to Attorney General John Ashcroft, who oversees the INS, as well as to the agency itself. We asked Ashcroft what he was going to do about the Malvo situation and the INS chaos in general. Here's the reply we got from Ashcroft's INS spokesperson, Russ Bergeron:

"If Bill O'Reilly doesn't like the way that Malvo was allowed to stay in the country undetained while he waited for his hearing, then he should work to change the law.

"While everyone says the INS did its job and got Malvo's fingerprints and generally broke the [sniper] case wide open, O'Reilly remains a voice in the wilderness, shooting his mouth off with only half the facts, and the half he has are wrong. You have a snowball's chance in hell of getting any comment from the Attorney General."

So there, O'Reilly!

Of course, I put the hellish snowball guy's reply on the air, and one week later, after tens of thousands of *Factor* viewers and listeners besieged John Ashcroft's office asking for some answers, Mr. Bergeron returned with another statement:

"The Department of Justice is actively investigating the circumstance surrounding the apprehension of Una James and John Lee

Malvo and their entry into the United States. It is critically important that the United States fully and fairly enforce our immigration laws against those who violate them."

Quite a change in tone, don't you think? But the truth is that every powerful person in Washington knows the INS is a mess and that millions of undocumented aliens are putting all of us at risk. They know, but they don't care. Most of *them* have bodyguards.

Think about this. What if the sniper had killed your husband or wife or child? Wouldn't you want John Ashcroft to do something? After all, he's supposed to be looking out for you; he's supposed to be designing ways to protect Americans. But what Ashcroft was really doing was protecting his own butt. He was never going to reform or seriously investigate the INS because that would be too controversial. Instead, he arrogantly dismissed his critics until the heat got too intense.

A couple of footnotes: A month after that dustup the INS deported Una James and transferred the head of the INS office in Seattle to the Homeland Security bureau. I know I feel more secure. And James Ziglar "left" the INS in January 2003. I called him up and asked to have a little chat. Ziglar said he was too busy *forever*. Another example of a guy whose salary was paid by the taxpayers, who did a terrible job, and who feels he does not need to answer any questions about his government service. Ziglar is a weasel, and an incompetent one at that.

There is no question that the INS is primarily responsible for the immigration mess. Even Congress knows it. In April 2002 the House voted an astounding 405 to 9 to abolish the INS and replace it with an agency under the supervision of the Homeland

Security office. A good start. But that legislation was buried in the Senate. Led by Senators Edward Kennedy and Sam Brownback, of Kansas, a Senate INS bill was tabled, then tabled and tabled again. Meantime, John Lee Malvo roamed the country and Americans died. Of course, Kennedy and Brownback will not comment on their lack of urgency concerning the INS.

They won't comment because there is no way to justify what they did. Kennedy, Brownback, and the rest of the Senate stifled INS reform even though a Senate subcommittee heard astounding testimony from the INS director of field operations, Michael Pearson, shortly after 9/11. Senator Carl Levin, a Democrat from Michigan, destroyed Pearson.

SENATOR LEVIN: How many illegal aliens has the INS released unsupervised after they were apprehended by the Border Patrol?

MICHAEL PEARSON: I don't know.

SENATOR LEVIN: How many illegal aliens released by the INS unsupervised had criminal background checks done on them before the INS set them free?

MICHAEL PEARSON: I do not know.

But the powerful in Washington do know. They know that the government's failure to control illegal immigration has directly led to the murders of Americans and to billions of dollars in related expenses. Twelve percent of all incarcerated felons in California are illegal aliens. The damage inflicted on America by uncontrolled immigration is incalculable.

Despite the documented danger, the federal government, for political reasons, will not secure the borders. Presidents Reagan, Bush, Clinton, and now Bush the younger all were given data on a regular basis showing that our porous southern border was a huge security problem. Thousands of tons of hard drugs and millions of undocumented aliens have poured in from Mexico while our leaders in Washington stood by and did little or nothing to alleviate the problem. Both Republicans and Democrats want the Hispanic vote and fear any tough action on the Mexican border will put that vote in jeopardy.

The solution, of course, is to assign the military to back up the Border Patrol. A Fox News/Opinion Dynamics poll taken in June 2002 showed that a whopping 79 percent of Americans favored a military presence to secure the borders. Just 15 percent were opposed.

Yet on January 31, 2003, at 5 P.M. on a Friday afternoon, the INS released statistics admitting it could not account for more than 8 *million* illegal aliens. The agency made the announcement verbally as the weekend began, hoping the news agencies would miss it. And most of them did. Except for *The Factor* and a few wire services, nobody reported the story.

The chaotic border problem and the Malvo situation are the most vivid examples I have seen so far of how the federal government does not look out for its citizens. There are no two sides to this story. The feds are not looking out for you or your family. And that is the truth.

What can we do about it? Very little. By law you can't sue the federal government, and if you annoy it, bad things may happen to you. I advise everyone not to fight the IRS or any other government agency. Just pay the damn bill. Hire an accountant to make your case to the IRS, and immediately hire a lawyer if another federal agency taps on your window. But never, ever, go up against any government official alone. They can and will hurt you.

Certain people, like Jesse Jackson and me, are exempt from this rule. I have a daily TV and radio program, so I can embarrass the bastards. Nevertheless, I was audited three years in a row during the Clinton administration. The audits were not specifically targeted, just big fishing expeditions. I gritted my teeth and gave the auditors an avalanche of receipts. I had to pay a few bucks, but I didn't back down from the IRS.

Of course, the Reverend Jackson is a different matter. He can do what he wants with his tax-exempt organizations because the federal government truly fears the man. No administration wants the racist tag he will hang around the neck of anyone who investigates or even criticizes him. Jackson is one of the few Americans who get a pass from the feds. If you want specifics about his financial shenanigans, they are documented in Chapter Eight of my second book, *The No Spin Zone*.

I'M GOING TO wrap up this chapter with some "looking out for you" profiles of government figures, but before I do that, one final word on our political system. After visiting fifty-eight nations, I still think America is the best country in the world. We have more options and more freedom to pursue happiness than people anywhere else on earth. On the other hand, almost every other industrialized country will take better care of you. Canada, France, Germany, the Scandinavian countries, and Britain all have elaborate entitlements for their citizens, and even for illegal immigrants who manage to get into those countries. But the entitlements come with a steep price tag: Most people in those countries will never become wealthy and independent. And most can't even choose their medical and educational providers. Taxes are huge, and so are the waiting lists for medical treatment and decent housing.

Therefore, if you are looking for a centralized government to "provide" for you, the U.S.A. is not really your place despite whatever Hillary Clinton and other liberal Democrats may promise. The Founding Fathers would have sent Mrs. Clinton back to Yale in an oxcart if she had proposed her vision of a massive central government way back in 1776 Philadelphia. The Founders wanted little governmental interference in the lives of Americans, because that's the system most colonists had fled in Europe.

But the minimalist-federal-government concept embraced by most of the Founders is anathema to many of today's politicians who want to be your sugar daddy, your personal Dr. Phil. Most of them swear they are looking out for you with a vengeance. Sure, and I'm Barbra Streisand. (By the way, if you are in need of a few chuckles, check out barbrastreisand.com. It's a real riot, Alice. Did you know that Barbra hired her own foreign policy adviser? No, it wasn't Alec Baldwin.)

And speaking of famous people, here are some big-name political power brokers and my take on their "looking out for you" résumés. Once again, please keep in mind that I could be wrong about these folks. But at this point I'm comfortable with the following assessments.

UNLIKE SOME FORMER presidents, George W. Bush genuinely likes people and would help you, I believe, if you could get his attention. But Mr. Bush is not a micro kind of guy—he leaves most details to steely-eyed assistants who will not be getting the Dr. Tom Dooley Medal for compassion anytime soon. The President is not a reformer, nor does he get very upset about injustice in our society. He is a child of privilege and brings a sense of entitlement to his job.

That being said, President Bush genuinely felt deeply for the victims of 9/11 and personalized the attack so that America's reply was swift and strong. If you remember the look on his face in Tampa when White House Chief of Staff Andrew Card told him about the murders, you saw a man shocked and shaken. That was exactly the reaction the country needed. It was personal. Bush rose to the occasion and was looking out for us by aggressively bringing the fight to our enemies.

But don't expect the President to challenge the establishment or initiate societal change. He's not built for it. He's not a problem solver, nor is he a risk taker. His appointees are basically ideologues and Republican Party loyalists, not brilliant innovators. Mr. Bush does care about people, in my opinion, and takes his job as the nation's leader with a seriousness that many pundits fail to recognize. But he simply doesn't have the fire in the belly to right institutional wrongs and demand creative change.

The most striking example of George W. Bush's philosophy of governance is his request for executive privilege in the federal investigation of former president Clinton's pardon of tax cheat Marc Rich. As you may know, Rich was indicted for evading $48 million in federal taxes and selling illegal oil to America's enemy, Iran. But before his trial he bolted to Switzerland, obviously to avoid a long prison term. Mr. Clinton, against the advice of most of his advisers, pardoned the unrepentant fugitive Rich in the last hours of his presidency but somehow never got around to explaining his rationale for that pardon. And since Marc Rich is one of the worst tax cheats in the history of the United States and has shown absolutely no remorse, an explanation might have been a nice touch.

Subsequently, however, it has come to light that Denise Rich, the fugitive's former wife, gave Mr. Clinton's library in Little Rock and the Democratic Party close to $1 million in cash. And Ms. Rich's wealthy friend Beth Dozoretz, a major contributor to Hillary Clinton's senatorial compaign, refused to testify in front of a congressional committee investigating the Rich pardon, citing her Fifth Amendment privilege. Denise Rich also took the Fifth.

Now, even Barney Fife could figure out that something is not kosher here, and indeed, the Justice Department is supposed to be investigating the matter. But after two years, nothing had been made public, and in August 2002 Mr. Bush announced he wanted all presidential pardon records kept secret for seventy-five years. This is yet another very vivid example of how the powerful protect each other. The Democrats owe Mr. Bush *big* on this one. Of course the regular folks, who would be chopping rocks if they ever pulled what Marc Rich did, get shafted because apparent big-time corruption is again left undisturbed.

Summing up, I believe George W. Bush is personally honest but is also a charter member of the power-establishment club that plays by its own rules. To his credit, Mr. Bush has a vision he thinks will help working Americans. But theoretical caring and actively looking out for people and crusading for justice are two very different things. In fairness, no president ever became great after just two-plus years in office, and Mr. Bush was a decisive leader during the Iraq War. However, once again there was a problem with secret intelligence concerning Iraqi weapons of mass destruction, which we'll talk about later.

So the book on President Bush is still incomplete, but we do have a couple of chapters available right now. His passion for America is his strongest suit. His inability to right wrongs is his weakest.

THE BOOK ON William Jefferson Clinton's presidency, however, is closed. Like Mr. Bush's, Bill Clinton's vision does include looking out for "the folks," at least in his own mind. Glowing when he felt your pain, Mr. Clinton liked nothing better than to bask in the approval of the masses. He *wanted* to look out for you. He just couldn't *do* it.

Unlike President Bush, Mr. Clinton is a micro guy and knows

the inside workings of our government and its failures down to its minutest detail. But his two terms were remarkably short of problem solving. He will go down in history as the "bubble" president, presiding over an insane economy that enriched millions of Americans—but only for a few years. Then the economy fell apart just in time to greet the new president, George W. Bush.

Bill Clinton's popularity in the polls was primarily based on good times—not his achievements. In fact, the Intercollegiate Studies Institute lists Mr. Clinton among the worst presidents ever to serve, alongside such stalwarts as Franklin Pierce, Ulysses Grant, Warren Harding, Andrew Johnson, Lyndon Johnson, Jimmy Carter, and James Buchanan. I think the ISI's evaluation of Bill Clinton is a bit harsh. He presided over eight years of prosperity and relative peace, and for that must be given some credit. He also presented a populist posture that reassured minorities in America. I would rank him in the middle of American presidents as far as effectiveness is concerned.

Mr. Clinton does not rank higher because of his incredible insecurity, which caused the quest for personal success and gratification to take precedence over everything else. Because of his self-absorption and desperation for approval, he polled everything, even where to take a vacation. His core beliefs were based on data, not heartfelt, sincere convictions. And the Washington power brokers knew it; they understood that he could be persuaded to see anything their way if there was something in it for him. Think about it, even if you're a fan of Mr. Clinton's—what exactly were his core beliefs? What did the man stand for?

On his watch, working Americans paid the highest taxes in history, with the exception of World War II, according to a report from the Americans for Tax Reform. Public education collapsed, national security was compromised, and the nation embraced a social permissiveness not seen since the Roaring Twenties.

To his credit, President Clinton did sign the Welfare Reform Act, and crime did drop nationally in the eight years he served. The government also piled up a surplus of cash because of all the capital gains tax receipts that came pouring in. But in many areas exploding housing prices left working Americans unable to buy homes, and millions of everyday people became debtors because salaries did not rise with costs. So you can answer the question for yourself: Did President Clinton look out for you?

One of his 1992 campaign promises pretty much sums up Mr. Clinton's presidency. Here's what he said: "We can never again allow the corrupt do-nothing values of the 1980s to mislead us. Today, the average CEO at a major American corporation is paid 100 times more than the average worker. Our government rewards that excess with a tax break for executive pay, no matter how high it is, no matter what performance it reflects. And then the government hands out tax deductions to corporations that shut down their plants here and ship our jobs overseas. That has to change."

But it did not change. Bill Clinton understood policy problems and talked a great game. But in the end he did little to reform America. On his watch, corruption in the corporate world escalated until it exploded into scandal because law enforcement under Attorney General Reno was so lax. Not since the Robber Barons of the Gilded Age had America seen such looting of companies and exploitation of everyday Americans as it did under Mr.

Clinton's leadership. That corruption led the public, especially investors, to distrust corporate America, and the stock market plummeted. The financial community came under a dark cloud of suspicion. In Mr. Clinton's last year, the economy was heading south anyway. But the corporate scandals deepened the recession that is still hurting millions of Americans today.

Here's an incredible example of how the government often screws the working American while looking out for greedy CEOs, and it happened on Mr. Clinton's watch—although President Bush put the icing on this revolting cake. In 1997, a company called Global Crossing set up shop in Bermuda with a vision of laying fiber-optic cable on the bottom of the world's oceans. The boss man was an American named Gary Winnick, who subsequently became fabulously wealthy after selling almost $800 million in company stock.

One problem with that: Soon after Winnick sold his shares, Global Crossing went bankrupt and millions of people lost all the money they had invested in the stock. Winnick, however, recently finished renovating his $100 million home in Bel-Air, a swanky part of Los Angeles. That's right, the guy who presided over the bankruptcy of his own company lives in one of the most expensive homes on earth. So how could this happen?

We should all ask Bill Clinton's best friend, Democratic Party boss Terry McAuliffe. Winnick convinced him to invest $100,000 in Global Crossing, and in 1999 McAuliffe sold the stock and cashed out with an $18 million profit. Along the way, Winnick got to play golf with President Clinton and hang around with the White House crowd.

Winnick also hired President Bush the elder to give a speech and paid him with Global Crossing stock. At one time the value of the former president's "fee" had soared to $14 million. It remains unclear as to exactly what the senior Bush came away with in the end.

So Winnick was one connected guy, giving hundreds of thousands in soft-money campaign contributions to both Democrats and Republicans. That really paid off.

After Global Crossing declared bankruptcy in January 2002, the press reported that Winnick had been quietly dumping company stock for years while continuing to tout the company publicly. The Justice Department under John Ashcroft then launched an investigation. The attorney general would not outline anything about the probe and kept the entire matter secret, as he does with just about everything.

Then, on Christmas Eve 2001, Ashcroft issued a press release saying that Winnick would not be indicted. He did this on Christmas Eve, knowing that most of the press was not working and that news coverage on Christmas Day is almost nonexistent. Ashcroft tried to sneak it by America. Still to this day, Ashcroft has refused to provide details on how a CEO can loot a company to the tune of three-quarters of a *billion* dollars and then watch it sink *with no legal liability*. How can this happen? No comment from Ashcroft. Janet Reno and Bill Clinton must have been beaming with pride. President Bush may be straighter than Clinton when it comes to personal dealings, but George W. uses the same kind of rationalizations when it comes to confronting corruption in high places. Both Bush and Clinton protected the powerful, even when the powerful damaged everyday Americans.

Of all the presidents I have known in my lifetime, Mr. Clinton should have been the one who looked out for the folks the most. His Arkansas upbringing was as humble as humble gets. Overcoming a weak family support system, Bill Clinton rose up and became the most powerful man in the world. Surely, he knows the challenges that face working Americans. Why, then, did he squander that knowledge by selling out to movie stars, special interests, and easy temptations?

I will never understand it. Bill Clinton loved to hang out with wealthy operators like Terry McAuliffe and spoiled divas like Barbra Streisand. Those people would never have spoken to him had he decided to become a small-town lawyer back in "that town called Hope." As president, Mr. Clinton let the folks down, even if many Americans don't yet realize it. But I strongly suspect that Bill Clinton himself knows exactly what he did and didn't do. Every time he makes one of his six-figure speeches, he furiously tries to rewrite his history. But this, of course, is tilting at windmills, because the statistics don't lie. Bill Clinton is revered by many on the left in America for being the champion of the downtrodden. Some have even called him the nation's "first black president" for his sensitivity to the needs of minorities. But the bedrock truth about Mr. Clinton's eight years as chief executive can be illustrated by one tragic fact: On his watch black kids continued to fall behind in the nation's public schools despite massive federal spending.

According to data compiled by the publication *Education Week*, in 2000, after eight years of the Clinton administration, 54 percent of black students did not graduate from high school in the state of New York. In California the number was 41 percent, even with its lenient practice of so-called "social promotion." In Tennessee, it was 54 percent; in Wisconsin, 59 percent; and on and on. According to the National Assessment of Educational Progress, the level of academic achievement has stayed basically flat since 1992.

During Mr. Clinton's last year in office, the U.S. Department of Education spent a record $34 *billion* on education. In Washington, D.C., one of the nation's worst school districts, spending on public school students is $10,000 per student. The student-teacher ratio is 14 to 1, well below the average for public education.

An interesting comparative sidebar: D.C. Catholic schools spend $3,500 per pupil and have much larger classes, but their test scores are higher. That proves that parental involvement and campus discipline, not higher government spending, are the keys to academic success.

Nevertheless, big-spender politicians continue to pound the drum for more and more tax dollars. It is a brutal shell game that hides the real reason the American public school system has collapsed: Standards and discipline are not imposed and the self-esteem crowd has won the educational war.

My one meeting with Bill Clinton, which I write about here for the first time, solidified my opinion of him. You be the judge. Two months after 9/11, I received a call one afternoon from Roger Ailes, my boss at Fox News Channel. He'd been invited to a swanky party thrown by Tina Brown but, at the last minute, had been detained. At that time Ms. Brown was one of the hottest media celebrities in Manhattan, widely written about as she launched *Talk* magazine (which would eventually fail) after editing *Vanity Fair* and *The New Yorker*. Her posh town house on Sutton Place was a coveted A-list destination. Naturally, Roger felt that someone from Fox should show the flag as courtesy in response to the invitation. Perhaps with an air of mischief, he asked me to fill in for him.

Now, I rarely go to parties, primarily because I am not often invited. I think we all know why. Also, I'm not much of a schmoozer unless you look like Halle Berry. But I did Roger the favor and swaggered on over to Tina's place.

When I arrived, swells aplenty filled the hallways and living rooms. Many affluent eyes narrowed at the sight of your humble correspondent. So I decided to seek out my hostess in a hurry, pay my respects, and hightail it back to Burger King, where I belong. Walking somewhat quickly, I turned a corner and nearly smacked right into Bill Clinton, who was holding court with at least a dozen of New York's wealthiest. No one named Vinnie was in the room. But I was. All conversation immediately ceased as the former president and I stood eye to eye. Seizing the moment, I extended my hand and said, "Nice to finally meet you, Mr. President. I'm Bill O'Reilly." (I guess I could have said, "I'm your worst nightmare, Bill O'Reilly," but after all, it was a party.)

I swear, Secret Service guys were closing in when the former president grabbed my hand, shook it, and then led me over to a corner out of earshot of the amazed crowd. Believe me when I tell you I had no idea what this was all about. But I figured if he roughed me up, it would make the papers and my ratings would soar.

But nothing remotely like that happened. Out of the blue and with no preamble, Bill Clinton proceeded to explain to me that he did everything he could to get Bin Laden. He said that every time he got intelligence on Osama, he acted. The son of a bitch (my term) was just lucky. The cruise missiles launched at the Al Qaeda camp in Afghanistan, Clinton said, missed the villain by minutes.

Our conversation lasted maybe two minutes. The former president was intense and engaging. I didn't say a damned thing, which for me is some kind of miracle. When he was finished, I simply said: "Good talking with you, Mr. President. Good luck." And I meant it.

One interesting footnote: Before Bill Clinton signed on with *60 Minutes* as a commentator, I was told by a guy who is in a position to know that CBS brass floated my name as a possible debating partner for him. Apparently the former president found that prospect, well, let's say, unappealing. I'll leave it to you to speculate about the reason.

As I've said, I believe Bill Clinton knows his legacy is shaky and is very concerned about it. So concerned that he has become a regular on the soft chat shows like the one Larry King hosts. The problem is that Clinton never addresses the three enormous problems he handed off to the Bush administration.

1. On his watch, Al Qaeda grew in ferocity and power. We've already documented why.
2. During Mr. Clinton's administration North Korea cheated on a nuclear treaty brokered by the U.S.A., and now we are facing a serious problem. Mr. Clinton says he didn't know about the cheating, but a 1999 article in the *Washington Post* documented it quite clearly. Did the President not read the paper?

3. The economic recession began in Mr. Clinton's last year in office and has been exacerbated by the war on terror and Iraq. To be fair, after the stock market bubble of the '90s, no president could have avoided an economic pullback. But it is a fact that, overall, Mr. Clinton handed one big mess to Mr. Bush.

In the future, Bill Clinton could be facing a bit more than a legacy problem. The people Clinton has looking out for him at this moment are in place because of his power and money. That's not the squad you want. But that's the squad that's available if you yourself are seduced by those two things. William Jefferson Clinton has accomplished what few men in history ever have. He has captured fame, fortune (he gets $125,000 to deliver a speech), and power. But true wisdom has eluded him. Although I still wish Clinton good tidings, I continue to believe he is a corrupt man. Prove me wrong, Mr. Clinton—reveal the facts about the Marc Rich pardon and the campaign finance shenanigans! A publisher is paying you millions to write a book. Earn the money—tell the truth.

THE TRUTH ABOUT Al Gore is that he will never get over the shock that the ultimate job has eluded him. The reason Mr. Gore is not, at this point, in line for the presidency is that many Americans do not believe he is looking out for them. And they've arrived at that conclusion because they can't figure out who this guy really is. Unlike Bush and Clinton, Gore never really let the public get to know him. Instead, he hid behind boring speeches and stilted photo opportunities. He avoided answering many pertinent questions and dodged explaining unpleasant mistakes like taking illegal campaign donations at that California Buddhist temple, which he did and there's no question about it.

If you saw Mr. Gore on *Saturday Night Live* or *Letterman*, you know the man can be engaging and funny. He does have a personality. But in most public appearances he's afraid to show it.

Dick Morris, who knows Gore well, said on *The O'Reilly Factor* that the former vice president is stiff and cautious because he lacks confidence. Morris points to the Democratic convention in 1996 when Gore was offered a speech in prime time. Morris, at that time a White House political adviser, says he was thrilled and his office began preparing all kinds of things for the speech. But Gore abruptly turned the opportunity down. Morris says he and everybody else in the White House were stunned. Why would Al Gore pass up a nationwide prime-time speech? So Morris asked him. Gore hemmed and hawed, but the bottom line, according to Morris, was that the Vice President felt he might not be able to pull it off. He was afraid he would bomb and his critics would toast him.

In the presidential campaign of 2000, Gore would not agree to come on *The O'Reilly Factor,* and I believe it cost him big. George W. Bush did appear and handled himself quite well. But Mr. Gore was apparently afraid I would challenge some of his positions. Of course, I would have, but so what? True leaders don't back away from tough questioning. Gore should have been able to defend his programs and explain his actions in office. That's his job. If he had come on *The Factor* in front of 3 million Americans and impressed them with his point of view, I believe he might have changed a few minds. And that's all he needed to do in Florida or Arkansas or his home state of Tennessee: change a few minds.

Gore's reluctance was very curious, because I did him a major favor during the campaign. You may remember when he said that a young Tampa, Florida, girl had written him a letter saying her school was so overcrowded she didn't have a desk. Some ink-stained wretches in the press hooted and slammed Gore for exaggerating, as he had done in the past. But when my producers tracked the girl down, she told us she had indeed written to Gore and told him she lacked a desk.

It took the former vice president about thirty seconds to run out and tell the press all about what "Bill Reilly" had found out. A reporter corrected him and said, "Bill O'Reilly." Mr. Gore replied, "Yeah, and he's not known as a partisan on my behalf."

Al Gore was not exaggerating there either, but it had nothing to do with partisan politics.

My problem with Mr. Gore is the same one I have with Hillary Clinton: the inability to address simple questions. During one of the presidential debates in New Hampshire, a *Time* magazine reporter asked Mr. Gore how he could oppose school vouchers for the poor after he had sent all of his children to private school. Somehow Gore wound up talking about the environment or something similar. He totally ignored the question and, of course, that pit-bull moderator Jim Lehrer let the evasion go.

Anyway, I have no idea whether Al Gore is looking out for anyone other than Tipper and his kids, and they don't count in this equation. The most selfish person in the world can look out for his family, but it's you that we are interested in. Is Al Gore interested in improving the lives of everyday Americans? I'm sure he thinks he is. But he is Mr. Flip-flop, that's for sure. His positions have changed 180 degrees on abortion, gun control, and tobacco—three big core issues.

Politicians who refuse to give direct answers to simple questions immediately go on the "not looking out for you" list. And as you know, that list is a long and sorrowful one. But I still have some hope Al Gore will see the light. One week before he announced he would not be running in 2004, I received a call on the private line in my office at Fox News. "Bill O'Reilly, please," a voice with a southern inflection said.

"Speaking."

"This is Al Gore."

I was stunned. One of my producers had called Gore's office a few days earlier requesting an interview, but we routinely did that and got nowhere.

"Mr. Vice President, a pleasure to speak with you." And it was. For ten minutes Mr. Gore and I batted around the idea of his letting it all hang out on *The Factor*. I was my usual obnoxious self.

"Mr. Vice President, it does you no good politically to go on shows like *Larry King*," I said. "That's like calling your mom. How many opinions are you going to change on that program? Why bother? You need to appear on the tough venues. Look, Rosie O'Donnell came on my program and changed many minds about gay adoption. The mail proved it."

Mr. Gore listened patiently as I made my pitch. I got the feeling he wasn't real sure what *The Factor* concept was all about, but I could be wrong. He asked specific questions and promised to think about appearing. Five days later he appeared on *60 Minutes* and announced he was bowing out of the presidential sweepstakes. Well, at least it wasn't *Larry King*.

But I may still get a chance to interview Gore, because I think he'll be back, perhaps in 2008. And guess who he'll be up against? Does the name Hillary ring a bell?

WHAT CAN I SAY about **Hillary Clinton** that I haven't already said over and over again? I mean, I have pounded this woman into pudding because she is definitely not looking out for you unless you are a member of one of her voting blocs.

First of all, Mrs. Clinton was one of the biggest-spending freshman senators in the history of this country, according to the National Taxpayers Union. This organization tracks congresspeople's voting records on spending bills, and our pal Hillary voted for just about all of them in her first year. There's no question she wants your money for redistribution under her control.

I find this strange, because Mrs. Clinton herself likes the concept of personal money a lot. She orchestrated her colossal $8 million book advance just days before a new Senate rule banned such baksheesh. Hillary's publisher, Simon and Schuster, a subsidiary of the mammoth Viacom Corporation, which owns CBS among other media properties, stuffed her pocketbook with cash for a book she didn't even write—she edited and approved the words of three other writers. (Admittedly, many celebrity memoirs have ghostwriters—though usually only one.) Could it be that Viacom is thinking about 2008 and the vast changes that are taking place in the American communications industry, changes that often need government approval?

Mrs. Clinton and her husband also took money from generous private Americans to finance and furnish her two luxury houses, which together cost about $5 million. She also ran up enormous tabs traveling the world as First Lady. In just one example of how Hillary used our tax dollars, she and Chelsea and an entourage of two dozen people went on spring break to North Africa in 1999. The airfare alone cost the American taxpayer a colossal $2.3 million. *The Factor* tried to find out just how much this entire junket cost but failed, because, by law, White House expenditures are sealed for twelve years after a president leaves office. We asked the Clintons to waive that policy so that we the people, who paid for the North African trip, could know the expense. Bill and Hillary, an insider told me, got a big kick out of that request.

If you follow *The Factor* on TV and radio, you know that this kind of "spend American tax money so we can have a good time" approach is grounds for "pinhead" status. I am no fan of politicians and their wives who enrich themselves at the public money fountain. So my negative assessment of Hillary Clinton is not fresh news. But of all the active politicians in America, I consider Mrs. Clinton to be the most dangerous. She has her eye on the big prize and she will buy as many votes as she can to capture the presidency. That means the people who support her will get massive entitlements paid for by the rest of us. I could be wrong, but I see Hillary Clinton as a person looking out only for Hillary Clinton and her daughter, Chelsea. Sorry, Bill, and look out, everybody else.

The straight skinny on Hillary is that she is raising millions for Democrats all over the country and will call in those chits in '08. She will pander to the minority communities, the labor unions, and the liberal special-interest groups. She will promise massive government spending programs to cure all social ills and, if elected, will deliver the cash. But she will never actually watch where the money goes, because that has nothing to do with her power position. This lack of oversight will result in tremendous amounts of corruption. If President Hillary becomes a reality, the United States will be a polarized, thief-ridden nanny state with a mean-spirited headliner living on Pennsylvania Avenue. Although Mrs. Clinton can be charming, if you cross her, it's the reincarnation of *Mommie Dearest.*

If you can help Hillary, she may reward you. But that is not looking out for you. That is *buying* you. And I, for one, am not for sale.

I'm sure Hillary feels strongly about me as well. After *The Factor* reported that she did not attend one funeral or memorial service for any of the regular folks who were killed in the World Trade Center attack, she told a CNN interviewer that she "felt sorry for me." Somehow, I doubt her sincerity. Call me cynical.

One final word about Mrs. Clinton: I get many letters from people who think I have something personal against her. I do not. But I see the Hillary thing very clearly. More than two hundred years ago, when America was an infant country, many scholars argued that the United States would never succeed because of its democratic principles. In 1787 Scottish historian Alexander Tytler wrote: "A democracy cannot exist as a permanent form of government. It can only exist until the voters discover that they can vote themselves largess from the public treasury. From that moment on, the majority always votes for the candidate promising the most benefits from the public treasury with the result that a democracy always collapses over loose fiscal policy."

Hillary Rodham Clinton has one and only one chance to achieve the power she craves so much: She can open the treasury to those who support her. And make no mistake about it—if this woman is elected President, she will.

While Hillary is the definite Democratic front-runner in '08, on the Republican side things are foggy. Only Florida Governor **Jeb Bush** has any name recognition—that is, unless the GOP adopts a Dixiecrat ticket and goes with Trent Lott.

As we've already discussed, Governor Bush was so passionless in the face of foster kids being brutalized in his state that it is hard to believe he is a "looking out for you" kind of guy. A Jeb Bush–Hillary Clinton race would be scary.

As for the other Democratic players in '04, it is difficult to evaluate their "looking out for you" potential, because they are cautious politicians who have not broken out of the pack.

I believe Senator **Joseph Lieberman** is an honest, hardworking guy who cares about the country. But if he's a trailblazer, even the people in Portland, Oregon, don't know it.

Senator **John Kerry** certainly has the résumé: Vietnam War hero, prosecutor, a presence in the Senate. But Kerry, after lobbying furiously for federal dollars for the "Big Dig" in his state, stood by and watched a $10 billion cost overrun. Your failure to supervise that project has to be explained, Senator, because that kind of massive malfeasance on a public project is hosing the taxpayers.

Senator **John Edwards** of North Carolina and Governor **Howard Dean** of Vermont may be looking out for you, but how would you possibly know it? Talk is cheap; accomplishments are what count. Edwards and Dean are relatively inexperienced on the national scene. But, then again, so were Jimmy Carter and Bill Clinton.

The truth is that our system of "public service" is no longer aptly titled. Because of the desperation of most politicians to retain power, they will sell you out even as they are trying to buy your allegiance. Holding public office should be renamed "service with (a) guile."

Finally, as I have mentioned in the past, the gold standard for public service was the tenure of **Robert Kennedy** as attorney general in the early '60s. His personal crusade against organized crime and the racists who were denying blacks in the South equal opportunity was stunning, a perfect of example of what "looking out for you" really means.

Kennedy, as we know, was a wealthy guy who was protected by his brother, the President. He didn't have to take career risks or even bother hunting down ethnic criminals, especially since then FBI chief J. Edgar Hoover denied they even existed. Kennedy could have adopted the John Ashcroft philosophy: Do the president's bidding and tend to the status quo. But in less than four years, RFK brought down hundreds of wise guys, including the fearsome and corrupt labor boss Jimmy Hoffa. He also opened up historical opportunities for southern blacks while putting scores of racist local law enforcement officials in prison. Along the way, Kennedy made legions of enemies, but that did not delay him for an instant.

Ronald Goldfarb, who worked with RFK in the Justice Department, put it this way in his book *Perfect Villains, Imperfect Heroes*: "[Kennedy's] experiences with Congress and personal sense of outrage provided him with extraordinary motivation. His impetus made his crusade against organized crime a priority of the Kennedy administration."

Goldfarb then quotes Walter Sheridan, a key investigator in Kennedy's mob-busting unit: "You grow up with idealistic ideas, but you realize more and more that you can never get them into action. All of a sudden the things you had thought should be done were being done, and could be done, because this man [RFK] felt strongly enough do something about them."

So how many contemporary American politicians have a personal sense of outrage about injustice, as Robert Kennedy did? How many of these people embrace bold, innovative policies that benefit everyday people? How many of those holding power in the U.S.A. right now . . . are really looking out for you?

CHAPTER FOUR

Your Right to Know

Stop, children, what's that sound,
everybody look what's goin' down.

—*Buffalo Springfield, "For What It's Worth"*

I **F YOU ARE** a parent, you should realize that **the media** are not only failing to look out for you, they could be your worst enemies. No longer merely content with providing sleazy diversions for profit, many large media companies have now embraced entertainment that is designed to coarsen children and glorify destructive behavior. Gangsta rap music, the mainstreaming of "artists" like Eminem, explicit video games that display every kind of perversion, "reality" TV programming that celebrates greed and selfishness—the list is endless. Meanwhile, the Supreme Court has even ruled that websites are legally allowed to display explicit images of "virtual" sex between adults and children. Apparently, the nation's highest court sees this as "freedom of expression."

Well, here's another expression: Wake up and smell the corruption. American society has become so nonjudgmental and profit-centric that it now refuses to set any boundaries at all. Kids are under assault from all forms of media, and it is simply impossible for parents to prevent cultural garbage from being dropped on them from all sides.

LET'S TAKE A very subtle example of how the media shape values. This illustration stars two divas, Whitney Houston and Jennifer Lopez, who have been shoved down our throats by a lazy and corrupt press. These two singers dominated the entertainment headlines in 2002 not for any special talent they displayed but for their turbulent personal lives. A gaunt Ms. Houston admitted to a perplexed Diane Sawyer on national television that she has a "bad habit" involving a variety of intoxicating substances, including cocaine. And Ms. Lopez, at age thirty-three, is a serial bride who uses her love affairs to garner publicity.

Now, in a sane society these two women would be chalked up as troubled souls worthy of only passing mention and perhaps some sympathy. But to the scandal-obsessed American press, these ladies are huge stars deserving of hour-long television interviews and glossy magazine covers. Of course, the public is also partially to blame, because we eat up this kind of stuff.

And young children are tapped in to this information flow. It was simply heartbreaking to watch Whitney Houston's nine-year-old daughter appear on ABC's *Prime Time Live* magazine program after her mother had just told the nation that she would do exactly what she pleased regarding intoxicants, and if anyone didn't like it, they could take a flying leap. To quote the addled diva: "My business is sex, drugs, and rock and roll." Then the little girl's father, singer Bobby Brown, joined in the demented display, telling Diane Sawyer that he just used marijuana "every other day" to "smooth himself out."

What could that little girl have thought after hearing those irresponsible statements? Her parents confessed on national television that they are deeply involved with substance abuse, are not sorry about it, and will do whatever they want. This is simply child abuse. I mean, come on, doesn't anyone care about the little girl and millions of others like her whose parents are doing the same thing? Yet there was no outcry from the media, no editorial calls for Whitney Houston to be investigated by the New Jersey child protection people. Except by me. *The Factor* filed a complaint with the state of New Jersey against Ms. Houston and her dopey, no pun intended, husband. Many Americans criticized us harshly for doing that. After all, they argued, it's nobody's business. And who has the right to be so judgmental?

By the way, our complaint predictably went nowhere because the authorities are generally frightened of powerful people and allow them far more room to act irresponsibly than they would regular Americans. But two months later the nation learned that the child protection agency in the Garden State had allowed a little boy to die and two others to be starved and physically abused, one sexually, in Newark. That's just another example of how children at risk are almost defenseless in this country because society simply will not confront irresponsible and dangerous parents.

While Whitney Houston's behavior has a direct effect on her child and other young people who idolize her, the Jennifer Lopez situation is different but equally pernicious to impressionable minds. Unlike Ms. Houston, who is past her prime, Ms. Lopez is as closely watched by American children as any star in the country; in fact, she was chosen in a Gallup Poll as one of the most admired women of 2002. She is the highest-paid Latina movie star ever, but she still bills herself as "Jenny from the block," attempting to market her roots as a poor kid growing up in the Bronx. And that's fine. Poor kids in rough areas need role models and success stories.

But Ms. Lopez also exhibits a remarkable selfishness that is front and center in her self-presentation. She graced the cover of the December 2002 edition of *GQ* magazine and discussed her personal life with writer Lucy Kaylin. There was plenty to discuss. Ms. Lopez has been married twice for brief periods, conducted a public affair with rapper Sean "Puff Daddy" Combs, and then hit pay dirt with another tabloid romance costarring the actor Ben Affleck. The result of the dalliance was that she dumped her husband of just six months, a dancer named Cris Judd.

Ms. Kaylin writes: "Lopez smirks at the mention of her [romantic] track record. 'I've made commitments to people and done things that I thought were right at the time. I just follow my heart. You do what you do at the time for what you need at the time. That's how I've always done things.'

"About her marriage to Judd she muses, 'I think you're always a little surprised when it ends . . . but it's what I needed at the time. And there's nothing to feel bad about in that.'"

Of course not. Why feel bad about throwing a husband off a cliff to take up with another guy? Guilt? Come on. You have to have empathy for other people to feel guilt. You actually have to think about the circumstance of someone other than yourself. That ability does not seem to be in Jennifer Lopez's repertoire, which is full of lyrical life tunes about what *she needs at the time*.

Perhaps the single most damaging philosophy currently on display in America's media is the "what *I* need" attitude, for which Jennifer Lopez is the national spokesperson. Going through life using people for what you need will ultimately lead to your destruction. As we discussed earlier, quality people will not associate with selfish exploiters. Thus, in the end, Ms. Lopez and others like her will be left using each other. But most people, especially kids, don't know that. They see only that Jennifer is rich, fawned over, and glamorized by the media. Thus incredible selfishness seems to pay off, because Ms. Lopez has it all, at least in the eyes of *People* magazine. By the way, one of Jennifer's songs is entitled "I'm Real." Well, selfishness and callousness are real, that's true. But those attributes are nothing to build a life on.

THE FALLOUT FROM tawdry celebrity displays is that millions of children now develop their philosophies and make lifestyle decisions based upon false media images and the meretricious marketing of flawed personalities like Ms. Lopez. Think about it. Children get zero moral guidance in the public schools because pressure groups have terrorized teachers into abdicating their responsibilities as evaluators of social conduct. And as we have mentioned, many parents are simply so screwed up that they leave their kids to fend for themselves morally. So what we have now in America is a system whereby outside influences are the dominant shapers of how children think. And many of those influences, especially on records and in the movies, are extremely harmful.

Kids see the success of a Jennifer Lopez and say, "Yeah, that's right. What I need at the time is what I'm gonna get. And if that hurts somebody, well, why should I feel bad about it? Jennifer doesn't."

Trust me when I tell you that that kind of egocentric attitude is sweeping America like a blast of cold Canadian air. Because callous, coarse behavior is being marketed brilliantly and incessantly by huge media corporations, millions of young people are buying it and behaving accordingly. In the fall of 2002 I interviewed two New York City fifth-grade teachers who work in bad neighborhoods. They both told me they are routinely cursed by ten-year-olds, who also verbally assault each other. It is not uncommon for a fifth-grade boy to call a female classmate a "bitch" or a "ho" (whore). Could that have occurred even twenty years ago in the public schools? The answer is no. But today it's common.

Corporations like Vivendi and Sony, which market degenerate rap music, have their line down: "We are not responsible. The parents should be monitoring what their children listen to. We are giving disenfranchised people a 'voice.'"

But when you point out to the wealthy executives that the poorest children in America are often the products of broken homes and do not have responsible parents to look out for them, the exploiters have no reply. They simply don't care. They are making money from lyrics that encourage drug use, destructive sex, gun possession, and a staggering variety of felonies. Rap music also often denigrates women, gays, and whites. It is a potpourri of life-destroying, mind-numbing, moronic ramblings. And society has accepted it (more on this later in Chapter Eight).

I could make a similar case about violent and sexually explicit video games, many Hollywood films, and those reality TV shows that have one central theme: I want to win, screw everybody else.

So it is indisputable that few in the media are looking out for you or your children. As it stands now in America, the entertainment media are hurting your family by presenting greedy, emotionally flawed people as hot properties and cool stars. The message this sends to an adoring, immature public is that bad behavior doesn't matter. Morals don't matter. Promises don't matter. All that matters is fame and getting what "you need." Parents and teachers who do try to preach a message of modesty and personal responsibility are really up against it.

THE PROBLEM IS so well defined that you would think the establishment press would be all over this story. Well, it's not. Instead, it is sitting on the sidelines, head down on the bench. The *New York Times,* the *Washington Post,* and the news divisions of NPR, PBS, NBC, ABC, CBS, and many other outfits are scared stiff of engaging in the cultural battles that are being waged for the hearts and minds of American children. It is far easier for the *New York Times,* for example, to continue to pound the drum for higher taxes so that the federal government can mismanage even more of our money than it would be for them to castigate the entertainment industry, which advertises heavily in its pages. Plus, you have that judgmental problem again. "Gee, we really can't make a societal assessment about Eminem; after all, he's an 'artist.'"

The no-spin truth is that the elite media think the degeneration of American popular culture is beneath them and not very important. Pop music, dumb celebrities, Internet filth—that's not what the *Times* believes is "hard news." So vulnerable youth is being corrupted? It's a nonstory for the *Times.* But try to put up a Nativity display on public property at Christmas, and watch your back: The *Times* will be all over you.

The real reason the so-called elite media are not interested in the pop culture debacle is that it does not fit neatly into their entrenched agenda. Besides, raising some concern might upset some of the corporate chieftains who own the media companies. If you watch and read closely, you will see a well-defined editorial pattern in most press outlets. Peter Jennings of ABC News, for example, is very interested in foreign news. Ted Koppel, also of ABC News, sees himself as a statesman and his *Nightline* program as a forum to discuss government policy. Dan Rather of CBS News is a hard-news kind of guy. He likes facts that are unshakable and homespun stories about Middle America. Tom Brokaw of NBC News is more of a crusader. He angles to tell the folks how they are being fleeced by specific actions of the government. Mr. Brokaw also pushes environmental stories that are sometimes tilted to his point of view.

The Fox News Channel, where I work, likes to focus on traditional things that are either being challenged or being celebrated. We are the flag-waving network that looks to America's past for perspective. Of course, we also cover everyday news but usually with an eye on how it affects the working-class American.

Our chief rival, CNN, sees itself as the world's scorecard, hopping from situation to situation with a quick review of the facts but little cohesive point of view. Recently, CNN's corporate parent, AOL, has begun making big changes because the lack of "attitude" on CNN has hurt the network in the ratings. In the age of instant news access via the Internet, a bland reciting of the facts is obsolete.

The *Wall Street Journal* provides a conservative point of view that exposes the often unrealistic and idealistic blather of some on the left. The *New York Times,* the *Boston Globe,* and the *Los Angeles Times* are all proponents of big government, and their agendas are designed to promote the forced redistribution of wealth to the poor and downtrodden. These papers delight in mocking the narrow-minded fanaticism of some on the right.

PBS and NPR are outright liberal house organs, but don't you dare call them on it. As for talk radio, most programs are driven by the Republican agenda. And if you disagree with that, you risk being labeled a "wacko" or some such.

But the question continues to hang in the air like spring pollen:

Which media operations are looking out for you, the regular American who wants a good life for your family? Which editorialists are fighting for your children to experience a childhood free from degradation? Unfortunately, there are very few press potentates who give a fig about you or your kids.

I'll talk about some specific press people in a moment, but first let me quote from an article I wrote for the January 2003 edition of *Playboy* magazine (by the way, I was fully clothed while writing the piece): "The people who really run network news are moneymen. Profit guys. News is a major pain in the butt to most of them because news is expensive . . . also, controversy is almost forbidden on the nightly news. That's why you don't see commentary. The philosophy is don't rock the corporate boat, don't get anybody mad at you."

Since all of the network news organizations, including Fox, are run by huge corporations, and these enterprises are loath to criticize each other or themselves, you don't see consistent, incisive coverage of the damage that many media operations are doing to the children of this country.

On the newspaper side, many of the editors are so steeped in ideology and political correctness that it is impossible for them to make any moral judgments on social trends. Unless, of course, the trend is spiritual or pro-life or something that runs against their ideological beliefs. Then the papers will let you have it.

So the final act is this: Eminem, Jennifer Lopez, Whitney Houston, Jay-Z, Puff Daddy, the *Survivor* crew, the Bachelor, the mean guy on *American Idol*, and just about every pumped-up media sensation out there can do whatever the hell they want without press scrutiny. That leaves you to fight these ferocious influences pretty much solo. You and you alone have to protect your kids. And God help the children without a vigilant guardian.

ACCORDING TO THE POLLS, most Americans know the press is not looking out for them, since journalists are ranked near the bottom of all admired professions, right between lawyers and car salespeople. (By the way, nurses are ranked first.) The reason that we wretches are under so much suspicion is that we are perceived as being arrogant. That charge is tossed my way often. I'll let you make the call.

But there is no question that journalists, especially TV media people like me, are frowned upon by many Americans, and I understand. Despite my job, I am one of those Americans disgusted with a powerful press that refuses to report on the reality of everyday life in the U.S.A. We have an obligation to demand accountability from big corporations that sell trash to kids. We have an obligation to report on school principals like the one in Plymouth County, Massachusetts, who refused to publicly discipline two students who had engaged in oral sex on a school bus in full view of other young students. I mean, what kind of message does an educator send when he believes disgraceful public conduct is a private matter?

The fourteen-year-old girl and the sixteen-year-old boy who humiliated themselves and corrupted other children most likely got their oral sex education from the entertainment media (or

President Clinton). We have an obligation to scrutinize show business and so-called "celebrities" who behave disgracefully. We have an obligation to hold the corrupters personally accountable.

But we are not doing it. And because of this cowardice and apathy, the forces of darkness are allowed to go to the bank unchallenged and, at times, even glorified. Worse still, when some of us in the press do object to the corporate assault on our culture, we come under attack ourselves because the elite media never, ever want to be shown up.

I'm not exaggerating; if you follow *The Factor,* you know that I am reviled in many media quarters and also in Hollywood. You will rarely see an article written about me that does not describe me as "contentious," "bombastic," "blowhard," or "bullying." While that assessment may be accurate, couldn't they throw in an "incisive" or "courageous" or something like that once in a while?

Anyway, those adjectives are used only after the writer confers the label "conservative" on me. Why? Because in the world of the elite media, a conservative is someone who can be airily dismissed as a narrow-minded, predictable thinker. There are certain code words in the elite media's lexicon, and "conservative" leads the list.

In reality, I am conservative on some issues, liberal on others, and sane on most. But because I go after issues and certain people with passion, I am a definite threat to many in the media. To put it another way, I'm not playing by the clubhouse rules. If you are a press entity and you editorialize irresponsibly or misstate facts, I will make certain that the no-spin zone will pay you a visit.

This frightens the hell out of the ideologically driven media on both sides, and they have not been slow in responding. Just two examples: Recently I was savagely attacked by a loony left-winger in the *Los Angeles Times,* and also by a far-right editorialist in the *Wall Street Journal.* I mean, these attacks were *personal.* They went far beyond professional disapproval. Collectively, these guys described me as some kind of out-of-control sociopath. The *Times* article was so over the top that I challenged the editorial page editor. (Not to a duel, but that would have been appropriate.) I asked him to send me another example of a *Times* column that vitriolic in tone. He couldn't do it. I guess I'm somewhat flattered that in the history of the *Los Angeles Times,* nobody was ever personally attacked worse than I was.

The *New York Times* leads the league in labeling me a conservative. In an article by Geraldine Fabrikant that ran in the *Times's* business section, the word *conservative* was used *four times* to describe me. That, I believe, sets another record for an ideological description in a single newspaper piece.

The *Times* loves to rattle my cage, and I must say I am amused by it. In the Sunday, March 2, 2003, edition, a National Public Radio commentator on language named Geoffrey Nunberg was lamenting in an op-ed piece that liberals had been "pigeonholed" by conservatives. Toward the end of his piece, Nunberg dragged me into it:

"But branding is a game that two could play, if liberals cared to leaven substance with style themselves. In their efforts to bond with the working class, conservative pundits can be as risibly phony and pretentious as anything that Hollywood or the Upper West Side has to offer. You think of Bill O'Reilly describing himself as a 'working-class guy'—this from an accountant's son who grew up in Levittown, New York, the El Dorado of the postwar middle class."

The El Dorado? Isn't that a fictitious South American city fabled for its wealth and jewels? Is this Nunberg nuts? No, he's just intellectually dishonest. Anybody who knows anything about Levittown is laughing in the aisles. Even the *New York Times* has to know this is stupid. But the *Times* doesn't care about silly things like that. It cares about retaining its power and marginalizing anyone who might scrutinize it. If somebody like Geoffrey Nunberg is available to do it, the *Times* will use him. Unfortunately, the marginalizing game is being played by many in the elite media.

LET'S TAKE MY PAL Bill Moyers, for example. Along with Charlie Rose, Moyers is the face of news analysis on PBS. And the man has done some fine work, especially chronicling how working Americans have gotten screwed by corporate America. But Moyers may also be playing a shifty game that is definitely not benefiting you, and he does not want to be called on it.

Way back in 1990, reporter Sharon Churcher and editor Peter Bloch detailed that Bill Moyers was using taxpayer dollars to fund programs for the PBS network. The problem was that Moyers retained the right to sell videos of these shows after they had aired. Thus, we the people were partially funding Moyers's private corporation. After reading the article, I came to the conclusion that he was enriching himself at the public trough. Since that report appeared in the sex-saturated *Penthouse* magazine, it's obvious why it did not get mainstream play. But I remembered the story.

Twelve years later, staff writer Stephen Hayes at the *Weekly Standard* magazine wrote that Moyers was still using public funds for private gain. That piqued my interest, so I asked Moyers to provide funding information about his PBS projects. He refused. PBS also declined to define Moyers's deal, despite the fact that it receives $55 million a year from the American taxpayers. Why the secrecy? Just tell us what's going on, I asked. But they would not.

Predictably, Moyers then launched a personal attack against me. He took out a full-page advertisement in the New York *Daily News* calling me all kinds of things and denying any and all wrongdoing. Because that kind of ad space usually sells for around $30,000, I told Moyers when I was finally able to get him on the phone that he had wasted his money. I would have given him all the time he needed on *The Factor* free. Moyers was polite but firm: He would never enter the No Spin Zone because he and I had nothing to talk about. Oh yeah, I have plenty to discuss with you, Bill, and you know it.

Moyers did, however, continue to hammer me at every opportunity. He told an audience in San Francisco: "I do not want to live in an America where Bill O'Reilly carries the day." Hey, Bill, I've got your airline ticket right here!

The Moyers story is important because it demonstrates how deeply ideological a so-called respected journalist can be. A Utah newspaper quoted Moyers as saying: "We [PBS] are not ideologues. Ideologues look at the world in a certain way and try to shape everything to fit that view of the world. I take my opinions and my views from the world as I find it."

Yeah, and I'm Ho Chi Minh.

Here's the truth about Moyers and how he "finds the world." Along with his journalistic career, he is president of the Schumann Foundation, which has assets of $75 million. Moyers doles out the cash and is paid $200,000 a year for doing the doling. And who gets the jack?

According to the foundation's 2001 tax return, Moyers gave $2 million to Tom Paine.com, which is run by his son John. That website is perhaps the most left-leaning enterprise on the Net. In 2001 it spent $800,000 on advertisements in the *New York Times*. Many of them attacked the Bush administration.

Bill Moyers handed out another $2 million to support the biweekly magazine the *American Prospect*, which describes itself as presenting "liberal philosophy, politics, and public life."

Moyers also kicked substantial cash to Ralph Nader's group and a host of other "progressive" operations, but no conservative outfits need apply.

Those are the facts, and there is no question that Bill Moyers is putting other people's money where his mouth is—waaaaay out there on the left. The fact that this man was a principal commentator on CBS News for years and now pretends to be nonpartisan on PBS is a joke. He is a committed ideologue who has done very well for himself.

And surprise, I don't begrudge him that. If Moyers wants to be a liberal guy, that is his right as an American and his privilege all day long as a commentator. But don't be telling us that you are objective, Bill. You're not, and your foundation donations prove it. And don't be taking taxpayer money to fund your crusade. It's not right.

In follow-up reports, *The Factor* produced evidence showing Moyers had received $769,000 directly from PBS to produce two documentaries that later were sold on video for his profit. Again we asked Moyers and PBS to open their books. Again they told us to get stuffed. But in the middle of the controversy we got an interesting call from a guy who worked for Moyers. He said that the "liberal" Moyers does not provide health insurance for some of his employees because it would cut into his corporate profits. Again, I can't confirm this, because Moyers won't open his books.

TV Guide got on the story and wrote: "Moyers says he won't get into a 'p—ing match' with O'Reilly because he doesn't want to 'end up smelling like' the host of Fox News Channel's *O'Reilly Factor.*

"Moyers argues that his company, Public Affairs Television, is no different than any other used by PBS. 'You don't see O'Reilly going after *The NewsHour with Jim Lehrer* or Ken Burns,' he says. 'The charges are a ruse.'"

Okay, fine, Bill, Mr. Burns detailed his arrangement with PBS for my investigators, and it is fair and equitable. So why don't you just do the same thing? Simply open your books and embarrass the hell out of me. But if you aren't willing to do that, I am going to remain suspicious. At this point I believe you are not looking out for the folks, you are using the folks. Prove me wrong.

AND THEN THERE'S the George Clooney fracas, which made national headlines in 2001, and the fallout continues to this day. Here's what happened. On September 21, 2001, Clooney and dozens of other celebrities headlined a TV telethon called *A Tribute to Heroes,* which was designed to raise money for the families who lost loved ones on 9/11. An astounding $150 million was pledged by grief-stricken Americans. By all accounts the telethon was a smashing success.

Since dozens of people from my town on Long Island were killed in the World Trade Center attack, I was acutely tuned in to the suffering of the families. Widows began asking me why they could not get in touch with the United Way of New York and the New York Community Trust, which were overseeing the distribution of the money. I said I would look into it.

What I found out was disturbing, to say the least. One month after the telethon, there was still no structure set up whereby any of the families could get information about the millions that were pouring in to help them. Another month went by, and chaos still reigned. So I went on television and asked the "stars" as a group if they thought they had a responsibility to put pressure on the United Way to perform better, as these families needed help immediately.

Only four stars responded: Clint Eastwood, Goldie Hawn, Kurt Russell, and the singer James Brown. Those four expressed concern about all the confusion and were worried for the families. But scores of celebrities simply would not say anything at all. Now, remember, I didn't ask these people to come on television to discuss the matter. I just asked them to call the United Way and voice concern.

After our exposé, the personal attacks began. George Clooney went on *Letterman* and called me a "black Irishman who makes up stories." I use that quote to open my radio program. Tom Hanks told the press I was raising the issue because it was "November sweeps." Of course, there are no ratings sweeps in the world of cable television, but I suspect Hanks's publicist didn't know that when he put the words into his client's mouth.

The hits just kept on coming. Jim Carrey told Oprah Winfrey what a bad guy I was, and Oprah looked very empathetic. Big bad Bill.

But then came another *Factor* breakthrough. The vice president of the Bergen County, New Jersey, United Way chapter, Lisa Rattner, came on my program and said that the United Way's handling of the donated money was "inhumane, undignified, and criminal." While the families were suffering, the charity was hoarding millions in donations and not responding to simple questions about future distributions. It took an insider, Ms. Rattner, to blow the whistle and confirm what *The Factor* had been reporting. There was no longer any brush in which the United Way could hide. Including the telethon money, they were sitting on about half a *billion* dollars in donations while the grieving families had no clue about what would be available to them.

Still, some media outlets like the *Today Show* and *Entertainment Tonight* refused to give us a break, providing a forum for grousing celebrities but not for *The Factor*. But finally the national outcry became so great that the United Way of New York City and the New York Community Trust were forced to hold a press conference, admitting that they were mishandling the situation. They claimed that things were improving and the errors had occurred because they were "overwhelmed." By March 2002 half of the money donated to the September 11 Fund had been given out, but the other half was being held in "reserve." That means that the United Way still controls about $250 million of donated money. At the time interest rates stood at about 4 percent on short-term paper. Do the math.

What the whole incident adds up to is another example of an institution not looking out for the folks. As just about everybody except George Clooney now admits, the United Way screwed up. But the fact remains that most of the stars involved in raising money would not step up and hold the charity accountable. Since those stars got good publicity from their emotional appeals, you would think they would feel some kind of responsibility to see that the money got to the people who needed it.

The press coverage of the story was fascinating. As I mentioned, *Entertainment Tonight* allowed celebrities to blast me and never asked for my side of the story. But *Access Hollywood* was fair and gave me my say.

Good Morning America was also very fair. But the *Today Show* was another story. On Friday, November 9, 2001, I was interviewed by Matt Lauer, who set things up this way: "More than a billion dollars has been raised since September eleventh to assist the families of those killed in the terrorist attacks. A star-studded telethon on September twenty-first raised more than one hundred fifty million alone, but some are asking why the money is taking so long to get to those who need it. Bill O'Reilly, host of *The O'Reilly Factor* on Fox News and the author of *The No Spin Zone*, created a firestorm in Hollywood this week after saying that celebrities involved in the telethon bore some responsibility for ensuring that the money raised goes to the right people."

So far, so good. Lauer's setup was concise and accurate. But I knew this was hostile territory. The call for the *Today Show* interview came in at the last minute, after we had done dozens of stories on the charity situation. Over the years *Today* had consistently turned me down for interviews even though my books *The No Spin Zone* and *The O'Reilly Factor* had both reached number one on the *New York Times* best-seller list and stayed there for months. It was clear that the *Today Show* did not think highly of me, which is of course their prerogative. But, suddenly, *Today* was interested in booking me. I knew something was up.

Matt Lauer, whom I've known for more than twenty years, is an okay guy and a show biz soldier. He does what he's told to do. Lauer greeted me professionally when I sat down across from him on a sunny November morning, but despite the pleasantries, I was on guard. When the red light of the camera went on, here's what went down.

LAUER: You've said that these celebrities probably took part in these events [the telethon] a lot of times for publicity reasons.

O'REILLY: Some of them have. Look, you do this for a living, Matt. You know how these celebrities are and their publicists. You say one cross word about them, and you're on a list. All we did on *The O'Reilly Factor* was say, Give us a statement. We don't need you to come on. Are you concerned about this or not? Four out of seventy responded.

LAUER: There's a good possibility that these celebrities are contacting the United Way, which is, by the way, the organization in charge of handing out this money—that they are talking to the United Way, that they simply don't want to participate in your show, isn't it?

O'REILLY: They didn't have to come on the show.

LAUER: They didn't have to send you a statement either.

O'REILLY: They didn't *have* to. But if they are going to go on and ask us for money, "us" being the American people, then they owe it to the American people to say, Hey, I'm concerned. If you don't want to do that with O'Reilly, then do it with Lauer.

LAUER: Is it your contention that something wrong is happening with this money?

O'REILLY: Absolutely. I'm not saying anybody is stealing it. I'm saying that it's in the bank getting interest, sitting there while most of the families don't know what's going on. There's no database. They haven't been contacted, and a lot of them need money.

LAUER: Well, from what I understand, George Clooney says that—

O'REILLY: Let me tell you something about George Clooney, okay? He's stunningly misinformed. He has no clue what's going on, nor does he care. Here's the deal. And I know this, I've been researching it for the last six weeks. The United Way is in charge. And they are giving money to other charities, not directly to the families, and they don't know what the other charities are doing with it.

LAUER: But when the celebrities got involved in this, Bill, it's not like they went to Bob's Charity Express. They put their trust in the United Way. It's a well-established organization.

O'REILLY: That's fine. If Matt Lauer raises money for somebody on the block where you live, you're going to say I'm putting my trust in whomever I'm giving it to. But if those neighbors come to you, Lauer, and say, Hey, it's not getting [to me]. You don't say anything about it?

LAUER: But what about the timing here?

O'REILLY: The concert was five weeks ago.

LAUER: If they were to start doling out checks the next day and that money went to the wrong place, you'd be screaming just as loud.

O'REILLY: You're being an apologist for pinheads. I know you have to play devil's advocate here, but there are *not* two sides to the story. Congress is holding hearings about it. The money's in the bank. There are no public service announcements to the families. There's no database for the families, and they have not been contacted.

Then Matt Lauer and I got into it on the subject of whether I was challenging the 9/11 celebrities in order to promote my book, a theory the pro-Clooney crowd was spinning. Of course that was nonsense. *The Factor* broke the charity story because it was enormously important.

The whole shoot-out with Matt Lauer was extremely instructive. The *Today Show* completely understood the issue but chose to pander to Clooney and the others because it needs them, not me, to generate the ratings Lauer loves to talk about. He asserted that I wanted my book "mentioned" because I was a publicity hound. Of course I wanted the book mentioned. At the time it was the biggest-selling book in the country, but the *Today Show* was not interested in talking with me about it. So I knew beforehand that the interview with Lauer was going to be adversarial, and that was fine. But as a courtesy they could mention my book. They do it for everybody else, so fair is fair.

But the real point is that after the charities broke down and admitted *The Factor* was correct, that mistakes regarding the suffering families were made, I never got a call from the *Today Show*. So I ask you this question: Were Matt and Katie and the crew looking out for the families directly affected by the attack on September 11, or were they looking out for the celebrities? You make the call.

Nearly a year after that interview, George Clooney struck again. In a cover story for the January '03 edition of *GQ*, Clooney told writer John Brodie that while the charity controversy raged, he offered to debate me on the Larry King program.

Before the article was published, Brodie called me for a comment, and I was stunned. How could this Clooney guy be saying this, since we had called him scores of times and he had dodged *The Factor* for a full year? Before giving Brodie a comment, I called the Fox PR guys, explaining that Clooney said we were afraid to confront him on *King*. We all had a good laugh. I then had our guys call the King program. No one over there would admit to knowing anything about Clooney's offer.

In the grand scheme of things, this is not important. But in a small way, it is instructive. Powerful people like George Clooney often feel they can say just about anything and it's true *simply because they say it*. This happens in the circles of power more than you will ever know. And in January 2003, Clooney's outrageous statements landed him in real trouble.

Speaking at a National Board of Review event, George Clooney attempted a witticism: "Charlton Heston announced *again* today that he is suffering from Alzheimer's."

When syndicated columnist Liz Smith asked Clooney if he had gone over the line, the actor was unrepentant: "I don't care. Charlton Heston is the head of the National Rifle Association; he deserves whatever anyone says about him."

I mentioned the controversy on my daily radio program, and the phones went crazy. Scores of Americans called in, angry with Clooney. The consensus was that the comment was mean-spirited and Clooney was out of control. To be fair, some of the callers were ideologically motivated, as Clooney had also called President Bush "dim" and likened his administration to *The Sopranos*. But I was surprised by how many women called in and said they used to like the man, but enough was enough.

By most accounts, Clooney is a charming guy who, on occasion, likes to help others. But he is making enormous mistakes. He was dead wrong on the charity issue. If you raise money for a cause, if people donate their dollars because you asked, then you have an obligation to see that the money goes without delay to the right place. If Clooney and the other telethon participants had joined with me and put pressure on the United Way, not only would the snafu have been straightened out more quickly, but the celebrities would have been on the side of the angels. But in

Washington, Hollywood, and the media offices in Manhattan, the powerful do not want to be told what to do—and the folks be damned. Ego is everything.

In the back of my mind, I think Clooney, like Alec Baldwin before him, may have hurt his career. In the aforementioned *GQ* article, he came across as a liberal fanatic. His 2002 film *Solaris* was a colossal bomb, and his directorial debut, *Confessions of a Dangerous Mind,* did not do well at the box office either. Something tells me Clooney had best be careful.

MY THEORY IS that once everyday Americans feel a powerful person is not looking out for them, that person's career is in trouble. I could be wrong, but the careers of Jane Fonda, Michael Jackson, Sean Penn, Woody Allen, and many others have cratered after their words or actions offended millions of Americans. The press may not be judgmental, but many American consumers are.

If you don't believe that, let's take a look at what happened to the cable channel VH1. That music outfit decided to air a series called *Music Behind Bars* in the fall of 2002. The premise was to have incarcerated felons play rock music in prison, then to broadcast the concerts and interviews with those criminals worldwide.

Amazingly, VH1 actually received permission from three states to shoot the show: Pennsylvania, West Virginia, and New Jersey. Both the pinheads who produced the program and the wardens who allowed them access to the prisons thought it was just swell that murderers and rapists would get a chance to be rock stars.

But many of the families and friends of the victims of their terrible crimes did not share that enthusiasm.

I got calls from a number of these family members and put three of them on the air. Their reactions were similar: Seeing these thugs on television is painful and reopens old wounds for the brutalized victims. You can imagine how a woman who was raped would feel seeing the rapist howling away in a rock concert. You can imagine how the mother of a murdered son would feel watching the killer playing a guitar and grinning into the camera. VH1 ignored their pleas to cancel the series. But I allowed these people a national forum in which to state their case.

After I aired the story, every sponsor of the program except AOL Time Warner dropped out. Thousands of angry Americans called or sent letters to VH1 and its parent company, Viacom. But the corporate suits would not relent. Despite having little paid advertising, VH1 continued to air the series. In one especially shocking episode, the network featured an inmate-rocker who had actually burned a baby to death.

Because of their gross insensitivity to victims of violent crime, I named VH1 president and CEO Christina Norman and the host of the series, actor Dylan McDermott, as two of the top villains of 2002. And villains they remain.

As far as I know, only one media outlet in the country stuck up for VH1. The *Pittsburgh Post-Gazette* editorialized that *Music Behind Bars* was actually *good for society*. They wrote:

"It isn't surprising . . . that the victims' families also resent the idea of prisoners being allowed even a moment of creative expression. 'Instead of singing and dancing, perhaps they should spend more of their time thinking about what they've done,' said the mother of one of the victims of a band member. That's a wholly understandable reaction from a crime victim's loved one, but prison authorities can't abdicate the management of their institutions to outsiders. The state can be sensitive to victims without denying prisoners the opportunities for artistic expression."

When I read that editorial I was stunned: This newspaper actually believes baby killers have the right to "artistic expression" while serving their debt to society? So I asked the *Post-Gazette* to explain itself on the air. Michael McGough, the editorial page director, showed up on *The Radio Factor* and was, well, dressed down rather heatedly.

McGough had made the enormous mistake of writing this: "Not content to accuse the documentary of glorifying criminals, [O'Reilly] had interviewed the sister of a murder victim. . . . But that wasn't enough. O'Reilly *allowed her* [italics mine] to embellish her understandable emotion with an implausible argument: 'In my opinion, watching this makes you want to be this person, because you're able to go ahead and, you know, be a rock star in prison. . . .'"

I let McGough have it right between his politically correct eyes. In full-tilt mode I said: "I resent the fact that you said that we exploited this woman. We gave this woman a voice. That's something that you and your stupid newspaper would never do, you pinhead. You would never do that.

"You're too busy making highfalutin moral pronouncements about how prisoners should be treated inside of prison, that they should have creative expression after they've taken a human life.

You see, you and your ilk . . . never get down to the suffering and pain of the crime victims, because you don't want those voices to be heard. The *Post-Gazette* should be ashamed of itself."

McGough countered with some incomprehensible nonsense about social responsibility to prisoners, and it was clear to everyone that he was not at all ashamed. In an article following his appearance, McGough portrayed me as some kind of raving madman and the folks who pilloried his stance via e-mail as the great unwashed. That is what usually happens in these cases. I leave it to you to decide who is right about VH1, but the fact that the *Pittsburgh Post-Gazette* editorial page objected to a murder victim's sister having her opinion heard really says it all. The media elite often think it is above and beyond the everyday folks. Intoxicated with power, many press people sincerely believe they know what is best for you and your family. And if you don't go along with that, well, you simply aren't smart enough to understand what "artistic expression" is all about.

Sometimes the elite media not only *justify* pernicious conduct on the part of fringe people, they actively *promote* it. In the Sunday Style section of the *New York Times* on February 23, 2003, a puff piece on a photographer named Ryan McGinley touted his exhibition at the Whitney Museum in New York City. The article by Carl Swanson described the twenty-five-year-old this way: "Mr. McGinley maintains that he is not about pushing buttons [with his photographs]. And although much of his work reflects his life as a young gay man, he does want to treat that matter-of-factly. His photograph of his friend and muse, Eric, masturbating, for example, might seem shocking, even deliberately so, but

Mr. McGinley insists he is really trying 'to make the sensational banal.'

"The same goes for his treatment of the beer and cocaine parties he chronicles. It's about the happy effects of the drug. . . ." By the way, the article is accompanied by a photo of McGinley asleep with some guy.

So there's your teenager reading the *Times* and he or she sees this. So I ask you again: Are the *New York Times* and other press outlets that refuse to make any judgments about appropriate behavior looking out for you?

ONE MORE EXAMPLE of elitism before I mention some media people who *are* looking out for you. Do you know Charles Grodin? He's a fine actor who somehow segued into the news commentary business with, in my estimation, dubious results. Grodin was clever on some late-night talk shows, got his own chat program on MSNBC, did poorly, got fired, and then surfaced as the Andy Rooney–equivalent essayist on *60 Minutes II*. Unfortunately for him, Grodin got the ax from CBS because his analysis was found lacking.

Now, I don't know Charles Grodin, have nothing against him, and therefore was surprised when he took some swipes at me in his recent book. He was angry that I supported a strong military response in Afghanistan after September 11, and basically wrote that I have the sensibilities of a Comanche Indian. I'm fascinated by attacks like that because I'm always curious as to what motivates them. So I invited Grodin to appear on *The Factor* to see if he could back up his poison penmanship. But he turned us down even though his book was going into the tank and obviously could have used some national publicity. So I made him the most ridiculous item of the day, basically chiding him for a "write and run" felony.

A few days later I received this e-mail: "Bill O'Reilly, with your typical arrogance you assume that I and others who choose not to come on your show make that choice out of fear. The reasons I wouldn't be interested in talking with you are very clear in my book. Why don't you address some of those instead of your usual name-calling? Charles Grodin."

It was a slow day, so I fired up the e-mail and hit the reply button: "Mr. Grodin, where I come from, you say things to people directly. I've given you the chance to do that. What you write or say to other people about me is insignificant. My offer still stands and a man would take it. Bill O'Reilly."

I figured I'd hit him in his macho pride. Didn't work. Grodin fired back: "Bill O'Reilly, as far as saying things to people directly, if you'd followed your own advice in the past I would respect that, but you haven't. We also clearly have a different definition of what a man is. Where I come from a man doesn't say about innocent civilians, 'Let them eat sand. Let them starve.' I'll take the last word on this one."

Aha! Grodin and Bill Moyers must be going camping together. The same spark that had fired up Moyers and Phil Donahue now ignited Charles Grodin. Here's the genesis.

Shortly after the 9/11 attack, I appeared with Donahue on *Good Morning America*. Diane Sawyer moderated, and the subject was how the United States should retaliate against the Taliban government in Afghanistan. As usual, my point was simple and direct: We should defeat the Taliban militarily, throw them out of power, and hunt down Osama Bin Laden, who was under the Taliban's protection.

Phil Donahue was against that. He wanted a "police action" whereby the United States would join with the United Nations and invoke "sanctions" against the Taliban. Donahue insisted that even if military action were necessary, the United States had no legal right to "go it alone."

I, of course, said that was insane. "Do you mean to tell me, Mr. Donahue, that our government does not have the right to attack a government that harbors the killers of three thousand Americans? Are you going to sit here and tell that to the families who lost loved ones to the terrorist attack? Are you going to tell them that we have to get Belgium's permission before we act militarily?"

Donahue's veins bulged as his face went scarlet. "What about the innocent civilians that will be killed if we attack?" he raged.

"That's war. If a government allows a terrorist group to attack America, that government has to be brought down by force," I replied. "I would not target civilians, but I would bomb the infrastructure of Afghanistan and force the Taliban out."

Of course, that's exactly what happened. Using airpower, the Bush administration quickly broke the Taliban. But to this day

Grodin, Donahue, and Moyers don't like it. I guess you could argue that they are looking out for the Afghan people. But are they looking out for you?

T**HE SAD TRUTH** is that most high-profile media people are looking out for themselves and themselves alone. On any given day in Manhattan, you will see them dining in incredibly expensive restaurants with other powerful people. You will see them at swanky parties and black-tie charity events. You will see them at their lavish vacation homes in the Hamptons, Aspen, or Loudoun County, Virginia. You will not see them at Wal-Mart.

There are some exceptions. John Stossel and Brian Ross of ABC News often expose things that are harmful to the folks, and Peter Jennings respects reporting that benefits working Americans. I know this firsthand because I was an ABC News correspondent in the 1980s. Even though Jennings sees himself as a sophisticate, he encouraged me to find stories that impacted working Americans. Sometimes Jennings himself had to insist that such stories be slotted in on *World News Tonight*. As with all network news organizations, many ABC News producers held a built-in prejudice against "populist stories." Jennings fought that prejudice and helped me immensely.

Over at NBC News, Tim Russert is a guy who looks out for the folks by refusing to pander to the powerful politicians he interviews on *Meet the Press*. Russert has to walk a delicate line.

He can't hammer these people as I sometimes do on *The Factor*, because NBC's parent company, General Electric, would not be comfortable with that. Nevertheless, Russert manages to raise the issues the folks need to know about and gets his points across, all the while grinning like a likable raccoon.

Mike Wallace and the *60 Minutes* crew in general know who the bad guys are and, at times, use their enormous power to nail them. But the crusading days of *60 Minutes* are over, and that's a shame. At its best, *60 Minutes* made those in power tremble. But Wallace is eighty-five and his boss, Don Hewitt, is also in his eighties. How many more corporate battles can these guys take on? When I'm that age, I'll be in an urn someplace. (Let's hope Moyers, Donahue, and Grodin don't have access to that urn. . . .)

On the print side, the *New York Times* can unleash some brilliant reporters like Jeff Gerth if the spirit moves the elitist editors. Unfortunately, the *Times* is far more interested in promoting ideology and political correctness (remember the Jayson Blair scandal) than in exposing corruption, and we know that the now-resigned executive editor, Howell Raines, allowed his disdain for the Iraq War to shade the hard news coverage the *Times* provided about the situation. In the first few days of the conflict, the *New York Times* was loaded with negative headlines about how "fierce" the Iraqi resistance was. At the same time, Fox News was reporting that the coalition was cutting through the Iraqi forces like, with apologies to Mike Myers, butter. Subsequently, Fox was proved right and the *Times* wrong. More on the war coming up, but in my opinion, the *New York Times* booted one of the biggest stories in decades.

The syndicated columnist Michelle Malkin, who writes about our failure to protect our borders, is definitely looking out for the folks, so her column is worth reading. The old-timers like Jimmy Breslin at *Newsday* and Pete Hamill at the New York *Daily News* can still light it up once in a while on behalf of the working and average American, but where are the angry, crusading young reporters and columnists?

Unfortunately, few of them exist, because the journalistic profession doesn't encourage that anymore. I guess I am one of the angriest journalists around these days. At least, that's what the ABC newsmagazine *Prime Time Live* put out there. When they did a segment on me, correspondent Chris Cuomo must have asked me twenty times, "Why are you so angry?"

"Because every journalist should be angry," I answered. "Reporters are in a position to expose corruption and deceit in high places. But in order to do that you have to be annoyed about corruption and deceit. If you're a journalist and you're not angry about social injustice, get out. Be a barber."

But Cuomo, son of the former governor of New York, seemed doubtful. He kept questioning me about my financial status, my success, my good life. How could I still be angry when I had such big success? he persisted.

What can I say? Corruption, unfairness, incompetence, obsequiousness, and exploiting the folks have always made me mad. No amount of money in my pocket will douse that fire. You are either angry about social injustice or you're not. You can't teach it, you have to *feel* it.

And that's the crux of the matter when it comes to the media looking out for you. If it's only about money, the folks will get hosed all day long by the media. And right now in America, it is almost all about money.

Finally, because *The Factor* had become such a big hit, the Arts and Entertainment cable channel did a biography of me in January 2003. But the producers of the program still, to this day, have no idea why *The O'Reilly Factor* came out of nowhere to dominate the world of cable news. Throughout the piece, the A&E people kept hammering home this point: O'Reilly always has trouble with management; he always causes corporate trouble.

But why? It is certainly true that I did not bow to my corporate bosses on my way up the media ladder. I also gave them their money's worth by doing good and profitable work everywhere I was hired. But my job is, and always has been, to report the truth *to you*. I assemble the facts, then draw sensible conclusions based on those facts. I don't care if the bad guys buy advertising on the TV station, if they are powerful people, if they are conservative or liberal or Episcopalian. If they are hurting the folks, they have a problem with me.

Of course, that journalistic credo did not go down too well with some of my superiors, but I didn't care; I constantly dished it out even if they didn't like it. Finally, I got to a place, the Fox News Channel, where management understood that having that kind of entree on the menu might capture the attention of millions of Americans. And it did. *The Factor*'s enormous ratings helped drive the Fox News Channel to the top of the cable television industry, surpassing not only CNN, CNBC, and MSNBC, but most cable entertainment programming as well.

In a stunning turn of events, a Gallup Poll taken in January 2003 showed that cable television news programs had caught the nightly network news programs on ABC, CBS, and NBC as far as frequency of viewing. In fact, daily viewing of cable news jumped from 21 percent of viewers in 1998 to 41 percent in '03. Over the same period, daily network news watching fell from 56 percent to 43 percent. Since the poll has a margin of error of 3 percent, cable and network news are now effectively tied in appeal among Americans who watch news regularly.

That situation is not pleasing to many at the networks, and the propaganda drum continues to beat loudly that my network, Fox News Channel, is simply catering to conservative Americans. But listen to this. The same Gallup Poll sums up Fox this way: "There is little difference in the self-reported use of cable news by partisanship. There has been a good deal of focus on what is perceived to be a conservative orientation of the Fox News Channel, but . . . we are not able to distinguish any partisan differences in the use of the specific cable news channels."

In my opinion, there aren't any. Millions of Americans watch Fox News and *The Factor* because they think it is worth their time. Period. And why do they think that? Well, a Gallup Poll taken in February 2003 asked this question: "Do you think news organizations get the facts straight, or do you think that their stories and reports are often inaccurate?"

An astounding 58 percent of Americans answered that they

believed the news delivered to them was often flat-out wrong. Only 39 percent were comfortable with the accuracy of the media. In June 1985 just 34 percent of Americans said the news was often inaccurate. The startling turnaround over a period of seventeen years is certainly worth noting.

Since Fox News is the youngest of the major national news organizations, perhaps millions of Americans have found a place they consider more accurate. Of course, only you can decide if I am being self-aggrandizing or if I or any other media person is truly looking out for you. That is your personal decision to make. And remember: It is tough to fool the camera or newsprint. We media people say plenty, but what do we really *do*? Judge us on that. And say a prayer for those ink-stained wretches and on-camera troublemakers who are truly trying to right some wrongs.

CHAPTER FIVE

God Help Us

Somebody up there likes me.
—*Rocky Graziano*

IF THE DEITY isn't looking out for us, well, the landscape turns mighty bleak, if you ask me. Faith, hope, and charity, the antidotes to evil and the forces of darkness, are so strong that all three affirmations are needed if civilization is going to continue. There is no question that religious zealotry has brought the world pain and suffering, but without the hope of eternal life, not to mention infallible justice, eventually dog-eats-dog turns into human-exploits-human.

For centuries, all members of the O'Reilly clan have been baptized Roman Catholics, whether the Church wants to admit it or not. (After my reporting on Cardinal Law the Church was not pleased.) From the time that I could walk, I've gone to mass on Sunday and have respected my religion. I am, I believe, among a minority of journalists who actually attend church on a regular basis. But judging by the stares I get when I leave mass early, I am not enhancing the image of my profession.

Since I have talked about my religion on the air, I am often asked by skeptical correspondents how I can hold on to such traditions, especially when I hammered the Catholic Church over the sex-abuse scandals (more on that later). I love those questions. Here's what I told the *Saturday Evening Post*: "People say, 'Why do you go to church?' I say, 'Why not? What is a better use of my time? For an hour a week, I can think about things of a spiritual nature in a nice church with beautiful sculptures and stained glass windows and a 2,000-year-old tradition that makes sense. Why would I not go?

"What's the downside of going? What if there is no God? Well, so what? If there is no God, I'm dead. It doesn't matter, OK? I'm looking at it like, 'What's to lose? What's the problem here?' If the theology is positive, if it is designed to help people, and I believe in that philosophy, why would I not embrace that? Now that being said, do I do everything the bishop tells me to do? Certainly I don't. He's a human being; he's not somebody who has sway over me. I can't understand that about atheists. Is there nothing you can embrace? Do you know more than everybody else and can you explain every mystery of nature? Why would you be so definite in the fact that there isn't a God? It doesn't make any sense."

I figured out early on that I was not nearly smart enough to understand the vagaries of the universe, so I threw in with the Supreme Being. Thus, faith was not a struggle for me. My logic is simple: Everything man is involved with is imperfect. But nature works all the time. It never breaks down. It never fails to show up. The sun comes up, the sun goes down. The tide rolls in, the tide goes out. Seasons change, people die, babies are born. Sure, destructive storms and fires descend, but new growth begins almost immediately. Nature is perfect, so man could not possibly have anything to do with it. You don't have to memorize Ecclesiastes to figure that out.

With the renewing cycle of life staring all human beings in the face, it is incumbent upon us to analyze things further. If Big Bang theorists are right, the entire universe was about the size of an acorn fifteen billion years ago; everything in existence was produced when that cosmic seed exploded. What human being could make *that* happen? Look around. You can build a table, for example, out of existing natural materials. You cannot create anything out of nothing. Not even an acorn.

If you are a nonbeliever, I respect that, but I also urge you to consider data from the scientific community. A six-year study of four thousand Americans at Duke University found that those who prayed regularly had healthier immune systems than those who did not. And it makes sense. Putting your faith in a higher power is a release; it is therapeutic, especially when things beyond human control, like disease or accidents, happen. Praying brings solace and relief. Trusting that things happen for a reason is a major stress buster.

Unfortunately, there is sometimes an element of "hustle" in the religious world, with various faiths competing with and even hating each other. This, of course, is absurd. I respect all religions that espouse goodwill toward men. I am not a missionary and will not tap on your window urging you to embrace Jesus. I believe that all human beings are equal in God's sight and all sincere beliefs that do not cause injury are acceptable under heaven.

Right away this philosophy puts me at odds with many who believe that if you don't believe what they do, you are bound for Hades. I could never figure this one out either. If a human being lives a good life, holds sincere beliefs, but just happens to be a Hindu, an all-just and all-merciful God is going to set the guy on fire for eternity? I don't think so.

It is this harsh, judgmental approach espoused by some true believers that has made religion in general a tough sell in the modern industrialized world. Many Americans and Europeans react furiously when a moral code is imposed on them. But sometimes the moralist is really looking out for you. However, it is also true that the more freedom a society has, the more difficult it is to listen to someone tell you what to do. Which, of course, is why Christian, Jewish, Muslim, and Hindu fundamentalists often do not embrace a free society, preferring the "my way or the die way" theological tradition.

So here's the question we are here to discuss: Does organized religion look out for you? And the answer is not definitive. Sometimes religion can be good and sometimes it can be bad. It is how *you* incorporate religion into your life that provides the best answer to the question. Use theology to help others and comfort yourself, it becomes a good thing. But use it to belittle and mock others, or to punish yourself, then it is pernicious.

In our personal lives, we do actually enjoy full freedom of religion in this country. But publicly that is no longer so in America. Because of the rise of secularism, a philosophy that argues there is no room for spirituality in the public arena, religious expression in public is under pressure from some in the media and, of course, from the intolerant secularists who hold power in many different quarters. They are *definitely* not looking out for you.

One of the biggest frauds ever foisted upon the American people is the issue of separation of church and state. The American Civil Liberties Union, along with legal secularists like Supreme Court justices Ruth Bader Ginsburg and John Paul Stevens, are using the Constitution to bludgeon any form of public spirituality. This insidious strategy goes against everything the Founding Fathers hoped to achieve in forming a free, humane society.

I said "fraud," and I meant it. Let's look at some historical facts. There is no question that Benjamin Franklin, Thomas Jefferson, James Madison, and most of the other framers encouraged spirituality in our public discourse. Letters written by these great men show that they believed social stability could be achieved only by a people who embraced a moral God. Time after time in debating the future of America, the Founders pointed out that only a "moral" and "God-fearing" people could meet the demands of individual freedom. That makes perfect sense, because a society that has no fear of God relies solely on civil authority for guidance. But that guidance can and has broken down. All great philosophers, even the atheists, realized that one of the essential attributes of a civilized people is a belief that good will be rewarded and evil will be punished.

In 1781, Jefferson said the following words, which are engraved on the Jefferson Memorial in Washington: "God who gave us life gave us liberty. Can the liberties of a nation be secure when we have removed a conviction that these liberties are the gift of God?"

I wonder what Jefferson would think of the ruling by the Ninth Circuit Court of Appeals in California that the word God is unconstitutional in the Pledge of Allegiance. I also wonder what ol' Tom would think of the American Civil Liberties Union suing school districts all over the country to ban the use of the word "God" in school-sanctioned speech. Here's how ridiculous this whole thing is: At McKinley High School in Honolulu, an official school poem has been recited on ceremonial occasions since 1927. One of the lines mentions a love for God. After the ACLU threatened a lawsuit, that poem was banned from public recitation, a seventy-five-year tradition dissolved within a few weeks.

This is tragic insanity. To any intellectually honest person, it is apparent that the Founders wanted very much to keep God in the public arena, even uppermost in the thoughts of the populace. What the Founders *did not* want was any one religion *imposed* by the government. Jefferson, and Madison in particular, were suspicious of organized religion and of some of the zealots who assumed power in faith-based organizations. But the Founders kept it simple: All law-abiding religions were allowed to practice, but the government would not favor any one above another.

At the same time, Jefferson in his wisdom predicted that some of the things he and the others wanted for the new country would eventually come under fire. On September 6, 1819, he wrote: "The Constitution . . . is a mere thing of wax in the hands of the judiciary, which they may twist and shape into any form they please."

How prophetic is that? Right now we have well-funded and extremely litigious groups of anti-spirituality people running wild in the U.S.A., and a number of judges are in their pockets. Led by the incredibly vicious ACLU, they are suing towns, school boards, states, and municipalities to wipe out any public displays relating to heavenly matters.

In addition to the Hawaii case, there have been dozens of other disturbing developments: In Georgia, the ACLU sued to get the words *Christmas holiday* taken off a school district's calendar, the antispirituality fanatics demanding the words *winter holiday* be substituted. But President Grant did not sign legislation making "winter holiday" a federal day off. No, he signed into law the "Christmas holiday." Nevertheless, the ACLU's bullying legal tactics succeeded in that case.

In Alabama, civil libertarians sued to get the Ten Commandments removed from a state courtroom. They won. You know about the Pledge of Allegiance suit in California, and I could give you hundreds of other examples. In New Jersey, the secularists even stopped schoolkids from seeing *A Christmas Carol,* based upon the Charles Dickens novel. The kids went to see some cartoon instead.

And the most insane incident of all occurred in New Mexico, where secularists demanded that the town of Las Cruces change its name. Las Cruces means "the cross." (It's still Las Cruces. And the upstate New York town of Fishkill is still called that despite the efforts of animal rights crazies to have it legally changed.)

What must Benjamin Franklin think as he looks down from Heaven? In 1787, Franklin delivered a stirring speech at the Constitutional Convention in which he said: "I therefore beg leave to move—that henceforth, prayers imploring the assistance of Heaven and its blessing on our deliberations, be held in this Assembly every morning before we proceed to business, and that one or more of the clergy of this city be requested to officiate in that service."

Prayers? Before a public debate? Clergy? Some Supreme Court justices are gagging on their gavels. And those jurists must really hate 1787, because also in that year the Northwest Ordinance was passed to govern the territories not yet admitted into the Union. Article III of that ordinance states: "Religion, morality, and knowledge being necessary to good government and the happiness of mankind, schools, and the means of education shall be forever encouraged."

Forever? Religion? Schools? Holy water, Batman! Does this mean that the media and the secularist judges and the intrusively dishonest ACLU have all lied to us? That's exactly what it means, Robin.

LET'S TAKE A LOOK at those Ten Commandments. Boy, the federal courts don't want you to see those on any government property, no way. But wait, there's a signpost up ahead. It was written by James Madison, the guiding force behind the language of the Constitution. Said Madison: "We have staked the whole future of American civilization, not upon the power of government, far from it. We have staked the future of all of our political institutions upon the capacity of mankind for self-government; upon the capacity of each and all of us to govern ourselves, to control ourselves, to sustain ourselves according to **THE TEN COMMANDMENTS**." (My emphasis.)

President Madison knew, as did all his founding brothers, that a precise moral code was necessary to set boundaries for everyday life. Ruth Bader Ginsburg and her pals want to erase those boundaries and allow those in power to govern solely by man-made law. But that is impossible. No government can police individual behavior on a massive scale. Either a society has morals or it turns into the Mongol hordes. The way the U.S.A. is going, you might want to start taking riding lessons.

It should be abundantly clear that the antispirituality forces in this country are on a tear. The trend began in June 2000, when a 6-to-3 Supreme Court decision held that a student in a Texas public school violated the Constitution by offering a public prayer before a football game. Interestingly, the entire student body in the school had voted on the student who would deliver the prayer. It was considered a great honor.

Writing for the majority, Justice John Paul Stevens opined in part, "School sponsorship of a religious message is impermissible." Yet a national poll on the situation found that two out of three Americans thought that the prayer should be permitted.

Chief Justice William Rehnquist, one of the three dissenting judges, summed up the situation this way: "Even more disturbing than its holding is the tone of the court's opinion; it bristles with hostility to all things religious in public life."

That is absolutely true. In every debate about public spirituality, the secularists spin the issue and equate God with the legal concept of religion. The two are separate, and here's some legal proof. God is a spiritual being. Witches and Wiccans are recognized religious groups. They reject God.

The United States was founded on Judeo-Christian *philosophy*, not a particular religion. As Madison pointed out, in order for a just society to exist, Americans must behave according to an established moral code, and they chose the Ten Commandments as a good model. That is the logic of the situation. A philosophy that citizens must love and fear a higher power and love their neighbors as themselves encourages civility on a mass scale. As I mentioned, the Founders knew America would never survive the challenges of freedom if spirituality was not a part of the nation's fabric.

Yet the spirituality and philosophy of the Founding Fathers have now been beaten to a pulp by the hyperaggressive forces of the secular opposition. They have waged a successful campaign to convince millions of Americans that public spirituality is "noninclusive" and therefore offensive. They have succeeded mightily in burying the true tenor of this country: That there *is* a right and wrong. That everyone is entitled to pursue happiness while receiving the protection of an effective and responsible federal government that understands the intent of the Constitution and those who forged it.

But why have the secularists launched their jihad? Well, the primary reason is that they do not want personal conduct to be judged. That's what this holy war is all about. If spirituality is encouraged in the public arena, then questions about violent crime, corrupting media products, drug use, abortion, sexual behavior, conspicuous consumption, irresponsible parental conduct, and a myriad of other personal issues will be raised. Above all, the secularists do not want that. They want a moral free-fire zone in the U.S.A., where consenting adults can do just about anything in the name of personal freedom. It is not an accident or a coincidence that as moral imperatives have broken down, the number of American children born out of wedlock has skyrocketed in the past decade. And that is the primary cause of poverty and crime. We'll deal with this shocking situation later on in Chapter Eight.

From their experiences in Europe, the Founding Fathers knew that a lax approach to personal behavior leads to decadence and decay. The Founders wanted moral boundaries and standards of behavior set at the local level. They did not want the excesses of England under the Hanovers or France under Louis XVI.

But tyrant Louis would love secular America here in the early part of the twenty-first century. Our dismissal of spirituality in the public schools and the embracing of secular values and thought throughout society would have greatly cheered mad King George III as well as loopy Louis and his greedy wife, Marie Antoinette. But America is paying a heavy price for letting the good times roll, a price seen most vividly in the behavior of children and especially public high school students.

I**N 2002, THE** Josephson Institute of Ethics issued an updated study entitled "The Ethics of American Youth." The California think tank surveyed twelve thousand American high school students and found a serious deterioration in moral conduct over the past ten years. Here are some of the lowlights:

Cheating: In the decade from 1992 to 2001, the number of high school students who admitted cheating on an exam increased from 61 percent to 74 percent—three-quarters of the high school population!

Theft: 38 percent of high schoolers admitted shoplifting at least once in the previous twelve months; that was up from 33 percent in 1992.

Lying: An astounding 93 percent of teenagers admitted lying to their parents. In 1992, the number stood at 83 percent.

Michael Josephson, president of the institute, told me that his study proved without a doubt that a willingness to cheat has become the norm among young Americans. Are their parents to blame for the trend? Here's a surprise: Josephson's study found that kids who cheat, lie, and steal say that their parents would disapprove of their actions. In fact, 84 percent of all students said, "My parents want me to do the ethically right thing, no matter what the cost."

So what's going on here? It's obvious to me that the parental wish is being ignored because the secular media and educational system often steamroll over parental advice. When peer pressure dictates that immoral conduct is acceptable, immoral conduct will rule. There is no question about this. And in the rejection of vouchers, which would allow low-income American parents to choose schools based not only on educational standards but also upon the moral atmosphere, the politicians have sold out our most vulnerable families. Think about it: Are the antivoucher people looking out for the kids? Or for the entrenched public school teachers unions and administrations? Roughly two-thirds of black American parents favor school vouchers. What say you, Bill Clinton, our nation's "first black president"? What say you, Edward Kennedy, often described as the champion of the poor?

The irony here is that while the secularists are winning the God-in-public-life controversy, America remains a very religious nation. We are not Sweden. A Gallup Poll reports that 85 percent of Americans consider themselves Christian, and some 70 percent are members of a church or synagogue or mosque. More than 90 percent of Americans believe in God.

And we Americans are active practitioners of our faiths. Sixty percent of us attend religious services at least once a month, while 40 percent go weekly. Add up all the data, and the percentage of those who feel that God is important in their lives overwhelms the percentage of those who don't. But the power does not lie with those religious people, who remain under siege.

In contrast, there is a kind of society where belief in God plays no role whatsoever, as characterized a half century ago by Whittaker Chambers, the man who blew the whistle on Alger Hiss:

"The Communist vision is the vision of man without God. It is the vision of man's mind displacing God as the creative intelligence of the world."

It was Chambers, once a dedicated Communist, who suddenly realized one day that the miraculous, delicate beauty of his young child's ear was clearly the handiwork of a higher being. He renounced communism because he recognized that "man's mind" could not be "the creative intelligence of the world."

But conversion anecdotes will never change the minds of the antispiritual forces, and the battering ram that is the legal system will continue to smash down public utterances and displays of spirituality until the religious population organizes and strikes back. Where is the AACLU, the *anti*-American Civil Liberties Union? I mean, come on, the ACLU drapes the Constitution all over itself, but a strong argument can be made that they are anti-American in the deepest sense—as outlined above. Their true agenda is a secular society. So my question is: Where are the countersuits? Where are the voices of opposition to secularism? Right now they are found primarily on the Christian right, which has been demonized, pardon the pun, as fanatically extreme because of its tendency to condemn its opposition to hellfire. Believe me, I know. Many letters to *The Factor* give me clear road maps to the devil's den—and suggest I'm headed there.

The unrecognized bitter truth about God and America is that organized religion is scared. The churches don't want to say anything that might endanger their tax-exempt status. They stay out of politics; they actively practice the doctrine of separation of church and state. But that doesn't mean that good people who believe in the presence of public spirituality have to stay out of the fray. As the Isley Brothers sang, "Fight the Power." And right now the ACLU has the power and is using it to pulverize American tradition and the true intentions of the Founding Fathers.

NOWHERE IS THE civil impotence of religion in the U.S.A. better demonstrated than by the Catholic Church. A whopping 65 million Americans are Catholics, almost 25 percent of the population. Yet the Catholic Church in America, which used to be a tremendous force for effective social change, is now on the defensive and, in many quarters, is an object of public derision.

Do you know why? Because the Catholic Church stopped looking out for the folks, that's why. Its leadership is made up primarily of elderly white men who have spent their lives playing politics and currying favor with the conservative zealots in the Vatican. Cardinal Law in Boston, Cardinal Mahony in Los Angeles, and Cardinal Egan in New York are all men of guile, power players who enjoy their wealth and influence. I could list scores of bishops who play the same kind of callous game—that is, amassing power and money while completely forgetting the mission that Jesus died to promote. In my diocese on Long Island, Bishop William Murphy, a protégé of the despised Cardinal Law, spent almost a million dollars refurbishing a private residence where he lives *alone*. I mean, Hugh Hefner would love this place. So who's Bishop Murphy looking out for? Not the parishioners. By the way, in order to secure his private palace, Murphy "relocated" some elderly nuns who were living in the building before he was installed as bishop. Unfortunately, these good sisters missed the new wine cellar and brand-new top-of-the-line kitchen appliances. Maybe Murphy will have them over for dinner.

With such leadership, it should come as no surprise that the clerical sex scandal broke wide open. With a few exceptions, like Archbishop Sheehan in New Mexico and now Phoenix, Catholic leadership in America is made up of venal, self-absorbed men who embrace the daily philosophy of "cover my butt." When Cardinal Law learned of abusive priests, did he leap up in outrage, throw out the perverts, and call the cops? No, he did none of those things, according to his own sworn testimony. Instead, he kept the situation quiet so it wouldn't hurt his standing in Rome. Thus his solution to child molestation by his priests was to pay the victims off and have them sign a nondisclosure agreement. Then he'd send the priest to rehab and reassign the pervert when he got out so he could be pronounced "cured." That policy, of course, led to the brutalization of hundreds more children, but did Law care? He dodged and weaved and attacked the press until finally the evidence became so overwhelming that he was publicly humiliated. *Then* he said he was sorry. But even after the crimes and payoffs became public, the Vatican refused to take aggressive action against Law and the other perversion enablers. And so the reputation of the Catholic Church in America arrived where it is today—completely down the drain.

The devil and his disciples are thrilled with this series of events, and Jesus must be weeping. He commanded his followers to seek out afflicted children and comfort them. Did Cardinal

Law miss that lesson? And what about Pope John Paul? Where was his outrage? In fact, the Pontiff even refused to meet with some of the sexual abuse victims when he traveled to Canada in 2002. (The Pope also alienated millions of Americans with his stand on Saddam Hussein and the war to remove him. We'll deal with that in the next chapter.)

The self-destruction of the American Catholic Church leaves the field wide open for the antispirituality forces to march in and do what they will. With the Church now lacking in any moral authority outside its own core, the loudest argument in town belongs to the freedom-*from*-religion spokespeople. And they are winning big.

FINALLY, LET ME tell you how my opinions on God and country were formed. My mother really wanted me to be an altar boy, and, for once, I went along with the program. Actually, I didn't have much choice because my father's six-foot-three-inch frame upheld this decision. He made the Supreme Court look like the Brady Bunch.

So by age ten I was assisting the priest in the Latin mass. Even though I had no idea what I was saying, I memorized lines like "*cum spiritu tuo*" and a myriad of other responses in the language of Caesar. As an added bonus, my altar boy stint was profitable because we got tipped a few bucks for assisting at weddings and funerals. And, hedonistic lads that we were, we quickly figured out there was good money to be made if the right methods were used. For example, the funeral home guys were the cheapest SOBs in town. I mean, these guys would scoop up loose change in an outhouse. Many times they would "forget" to provide the saintly altar boys with the expected gratuity for performing the funeral ceremony with dignity and compassion. On occasions like these I, having control of the incense pot, might become just a tad bit exuberant with it, causing large clouds of smoke to form over the grieving congregation. Of course, the priest would shoot me a dirty look, but the message was sent: The living must be taken care of.

Similarly, weddings were cash cows, but the mooing could be loud or soft depending on the groom and best man. They were the ones who tipped the priest and the two altar boys who assisted at the mass. One of the altar boys, always me, held the gold plate on which the rings were placed. If the gratuity was smallish, a small mention might be made of my sprained wrist and the kind of pain I would be enduring during the ceremony. Of course, the wrist could be steadier with a little inducement. It always came, and Father O'Malley usually got a few more bucks as well.

I never had any trouble with the priests, and a few of them were actually good guys. All the altar boys went to Father Ellard for confession because he was the local prison chaplain and, after what he heard in there, we figured our peccadilloes were insignificant. Father Ellard was also very, very old and couldn't really hear much. Obviously, this was a win-win situation, and even dastardly sins like making out with some girl usually drew a simple penance consisting of a few Hail Marys and Our Fathers.

We all knew what priests to avoid. One named Father Tierney

was a mean guy, and if you hit your sister or something, the guy could have you saying a couple of rosaries on a sunny day (rosary prayers take about twenty minutes to say if you slur the words). Tierney was also a boozer, and you could smell his brand right through the confessional screen. One time he really got on my case over an apple I confessed throwing at a car. I didn't even hit the car, but Tierney was going wild. "Do you realize this is the devil's work?" he asked.

"Sure, Father, he's zeroing in on me and some serial killers." That's what I *should* have said. Instead, I thought an evil thought about Father Tierney, thereby racking up a new sin even as I was getting rid of the old ones. It wasn't easy being Catholic.

As I got older, I saw differences between our altar boy crew and some of the neighborhood guys who had no formal religion in their lives. The differences came on two fronts: First, in my Catholic grammar school there were constant programs designed to help people and promote generosity. Even though my friends and I often mocked these attempts, the lessons were not lost on most of us. The sixty kids in my class at St. Brigid's School looked out for one another; intense conflict was rare. We didn't engage in ferocious fights like the ones we saw across the street at the public school. Generosity was part of the curriculum, while the brainwashing nuns pounded on us to think of others before ourselves.

One quick anecdote about the nuns. In sixth grade I got into a fight with one of the teacher's pets, a guy named Tommy Massey. It was just a little pushing and shoving, but because I was an everyday offender and Massey was on the fast track to Heaven, I took the fall. My sentence was to spend three days in solitary confinement in the convent—that's the place where the nuns live. I was given "busywork" and left alone all day long. The only supervision came from a housebound nun named Sister Gerardo, who was ninety-nine if she was a day. She was supposed to make sure I did my work and didn't steal anything.

I was not real pleased about the situation and plotted my revenge. On the last day of my suspension, I snuck out of my assigned room and saw that Sister Gerardo had entered the land of nod. She was actually snoring, a sound I'd never imagined could emanate from a nun. Seizing the moment, I crept out of the room and quietly mounted the stairs *into the living quarters of a half dozen sisters*! This was a major, mortal sin, but it was too late, I was there. The doors of all the rooms were open, and I remember everything was very neat. I couldn't tell which nun had which room, but I had to make a statement. So I walked into one of the rooms, removed some nun stuff, and put it under the bed in another room. I then tiptoed back downstairs.

Of course, I told all my classmates about it the next day. But something very strange happened. Nobody believed me, and I obviously couldn't prove it. So I did this bold thing hoping for massive adulation and *nobody cared*! And not only that, for the next month every time the teacher called my name I jumped up in a paranoid frenzy. It was agony and a punishment from God. But, interestingly, I never was called on it, and if I had been, I was all set to blame Sister Gerardo.

The second advantage we in Catholic school had was a structure born of tradition. There was always something going on. Our days featured adventurous stories about heroic martyrs and missionaries such as St. Patrick driving the snakes out of Ireland. There were Christmas pageants, Easter parades, and movies about miracles. As I came to admire the legacy of my religion, it was actually fun to learn about villains like Judas and Herod. We all admired heroes like St. Peter, who was crucified upside down at his own request because he felt he wasn't worthy of dying the same way Jesus did.

During my teenage years, being a practicing Catholic really paid off. I was kind of awkward around girls because of the occasion of sin it represented, and envied some of the public-school guys who were operators. But I didn't envy them when they got their girlfriends pregnant and had to marry in their teens. That happened to my cousin Eddie. He was always considered a cool guy at his public high school. He would die in his early forties from acute alcoholism, after struggling with the bottle his entire adult life.

This is not to say that self-destructive and foolish behavior didn't visit Catholic-school kids as well. It did, but not in the same degree and not with me (well, at least the self-destructive stuff didn't happen). When drugs swept through my neighborhood, I wouldn't dare and didn't care. I instinctively knew they were bad on every level. But my public school friend and chess partner Michael K. didn't have the same inhibition or point of view. He became addicted to heroin. He also died in his forties.

My saving grace, pun intended, is that I understood at a very young age that my religion looked out for me, and that Jesus was a good man. At the same time, I never, ever tried to convert nonbelievers, and respected the rights of every person to hold other beliefs. (Although I have to admit that we Catholics got a little teed off when half the neighborhood stickball team had to leave in the fifth inning to attend Hebrew school.)

Something about the boundaries imposed by my parents and my religion saved me. Many of my more secular childhood friends are dead or emotionally destroyed. Most working-class neighborhoods have a high failure rate. With my genes, had I not been born a Catholic, my life would have been much tougher. My religion, not any specific priest or nun, looked out for me because I took what was good and positive about it and used it as a shield. And I still do to this day.

Even so, I would not call myself a holy guy. I am a sinner, but I do cast stones anyway. That will make my meeting with St. Peter *very* interesting. Perhaps the biggest stone I am hurling now is in the direction of the secularists. Because even though my upbringing was rough-hewn, kids today have much more intense temptations to deal with. Beaver Cleaver has been replaced by Snoop Dogg. Children are under siege.

With no moral shield, millions of American kids will fail just like my cousin Eddie and my pal Michael. The secularists don't care; they want children to be at the mercy of a materialistic society and a greedy media. They want kids to rely solely on parents who are often irresponsible and self-destructive. Right now all we can do is pray for the kids and fight the secularists hand to hand.

And if you want some empirical evidence to back up that

opinion, listen to this: A study of college students seeking psychological counseling has found that their emotional difficulties are far more complex and more severe than those observed in the past. Researchers at Kansas State University studied students from 1989 to 2001 and concluded that those seeking help for depression doubled during that time period. Also, the percentage of students taking some type of psychiatric medication increased twofold.

That trend is not limited just to Kansas. In a 2002 national survey, more than 80 percent of 274 directors of counseling centers said they thought the number of students with severe psychological disorders had increased over the previous five years.

Now, you can argue all day long *why* this is happening, but I'll give you one huge reason: Many young Americans simply do not have a force in their lives that can relieve their emotional suffering. They are drifting away from our religious traditions—and religion can be that force, at least in part. If you are able to believe that a higher power will look out for you and will balance bad times with good times, your stress level will not get out of control. Religious faith is generally bad for the "shrink" business, but honest mental health workers know what's going on. "People just don't seem to have the resources to draw upon emotionally to the degree that they used to," the director of counseling at the University of Nebraska, Dr. Robert Pomeroy, told the *New York Times*. "What would once have been a difficult patch for someone is now a full-blown crisis."

The rise in dysfunction parallels the rise in secularism, no question about it.

THERE'S ONE MORE aspect of the religion controversy that needs to be addressed: the selective favoring of a certain religion in the name of "diversity." This usually goes on beneath the radar screen, but an incident at the University of North Carolina blew the cover off this trend.

I do believe the Founding Fathers were absolutely correct in demanding that no public authority in the United States favor a specific religion. So I was distressed to hear that in the fall of 2002, the administration at UNC was going to require all incoming freshmen to read a book entitled *Approaching the Koran: The Early Revelations*. The book is a sanitized version of Koranic philosophy, concentrating on lyrical stories and poetic lore. It's a very interesting book, but there's no way it should be mandatory reading in any public school.

Just imagine the outcry if any school demanded that students read *Bible Highlights* or *Nice Stuff from the Torah*. I mean, the ACLU would be setting itself on fire in protest—figuratively speaking, of course. But the ACLU was strangely mute when UNC issued its reading list.

So what was *really* going on here? Well, the backlash from 9/11 was hurting many law-abiding Islamic Americans, and the philosophy of "diversity" was taking some hits. So the University of North Carolina decided to set a proactive example and require students to read a book that is favorable to Islam. The intent was good, but it was a direct violation of the separation concept because it required students to learn about the positive aspects of a specific religion while ignoring the negative aspects. That's religious advocacy, not intellectual discipline. And that's not allowed in a publicly funded university in the U.S.A.

The force behind the Islamic reading selection was UNC professor Dr. Robert Kirkpatrick. On July 10, 2002, he entered the No Spin Zone on *The O'Reilly Factor*. I've condensed some of our debate, but the main points are these:

O'REILLY: The problem here is that this is indoctrination of religion.

KIRKPATRICK: No, it has nothing to do with that. It's a text that studies the poetic structure of the Koran and seeks to explain why it has such an effect on two billion people in the world.

O'REILLY: UNC never gave incoming freshman a book on the Bible to read.

KIRKPATRICK: We assume that most people coming to the University of North Carolina are already familiar with both the Old and New Testaments.

O'REILLY: But if you did do that, there'd be an outcry all over the country.

The professor had no answer for that. Soon after, under pressure from the North Carolina legislature, UNC dropped the book from its required reading list. *Approaching the Koran* became an optional reading assignment, as it should have been all along. And I'll go one step further: If the book was mandatory reading in a theology or history class, I would have had no problem with it. But forcing all incoming freshmen to read any book praising a specific religion does violate the mandate that public universities have to live by in order to receive tax dollars.

There's an interesting side note to the controversy. As I said, the ACLU was MIA during the UNC brouhaha (I love all those initials). Also, most other media did not cover the story as aggressively as we did. As part of our analysis, we rejected the argument that reading the Koran book would help us get to know the world that the 9/11 killers inhabited. Number one, I don't think the revelations of the Prophet Muhammad have anything to do with homicide and terrorism. And second, I reject the argument that you have to digest a book of poetry and religious interpretation in order to "know" your enemy.

I said this to Professor Kirkpatrick: "[As a UNC freshman] I wouldn't read the book. And if I were going to the university in 1941, I wouldn't have read *Mein Kampf* either."

Kirkpatrick asked why. "Because it's tripe," I answered.

The next day a number of Muslim websites wrote that I compared the Koran to *Mein Kampf*, the usual vile propaganda some of these sites spew out. What can you do?

IT SHOULD BE obvious to clear-thinking Americans that spirituality and Judeo-Christian philosophy were main ingredients in the dense fabric of ideas that became the Constitution. Simply put, historical revisionists and antireligious fanatics are tearing down what the Founders relied upon: moral clarity. And the courts are allowing them to get away with it, proving that the courts are not looking out for you, the American citizen.

As far as your personal religious conviction, that is completely up to you. But I will say this: Used in the correct way, religion can be a force that makes your life more worthwhile. It can make the bad times bearable and the good times more satisfying. Spirituality looks out for you because it brings you out of yourself and into a realm where the welfare of other people becomes as important as your own. And as we've discussed previously, that kind of worldview will allow you to build relationships with people who will indeed look out for you even as you are looking out for them.

CHAPTER SIX

The Holy War

War, children, it's just a shout away.

—The Rolling Stones, "Gimme Shelter"

ON MARCH 20, 2003, the day the U.S.A. and Britain attacked Iraq, the Gallup Poll people asked this question: Do you approve or disapprove of the United States' decision to go to war with Iraq? The answer:

Approve: 76 percent

Disapprove: 20 percent

No opinion: 4 percent

Gallup also asked if the U.S.A. should have waited longer before initiating the military action. Here is the response to the question Should the war have begun when it did?

Yes: 70 percent

Waited longer: 27 percent

Don't know: 3 percent

Overwhelmingly, Americans backed the action against Saddam. Yet on the same day, March 20, ABC News and NBC News devoted a substantial amount of their evening newscasts to both domestic and foreign war protestors. CBS did not, completely ignoring them on the Rather broadcast.

World News Tonight with Peter Jennings spent four minutes and forty seconds reporting on war dissent. *NBC Nightly News* with Tom Brokaw topped that; it spent four minutes forty-five seconds on war protests and another one minute thirty-five seconds on war objections by some Democrats. Neither Jennings nor Brokaw spent *one second* on the 76 percent of Americans who thought the war was the right action to take.

Dan Rather was smarter. He focused entirely on the war itself and stayed away from the policy debate. However, he also failed to mention the amazing amount of support Americans were giving the Bush administration at the start of the war.

If the goal of the network newscasts is to give Americans a balanced look at vital stories, a strong argument can be made that the opinion of the vast majority of Americans was blatantly ignored by the national newscasts on the day a monumental event occurred. But why?

The reasons are twofold. First, the visuals of protestors running amok are much more compelling than the images of everyday

Americans sitting in their living rooms, cheering on American troops. Protests mean action, and TV news loves action.

But the most compelling reason for the overexposure the protestors received is that there is sympathy for their cause in many American newsrooms. That sympathy is based on an internationalist view of the world that some in the elite media embrace. In their eyes, the U.S.A. should engage with other nations of the world—no matter how corrupt or tyrannical—in a "collegial" fashion. What's wrong with that? Simple. That philosophy does not look out for you, the everyday American, because it puts your security and concerns on an equal footing with the concerns of those abroad. And as we all learned the hard way on 9/11 and in the run-up to the Iraq War, some foreign countries do not seem to have the welfare and security of Americans at the top of their dance card. Does France? Does Saudi Arabia? Does Russia?

Since I can't read minds, it would be unfair of me to label Mr. Jennings, Mr. Brokaw, and Mr. Rather anything other than experienced professionals. Because it is impossible to know the thought process of any newscast anchor or producer, any analysis of their motivations would be speculative and unfair. I can report only what these men presented to the nation on the first day of the war. To be candid, *The Factor* covered the protests as well, but not as the fighting in Iraq commenced, and our coverage of the dissenters was certainly far more skeptical as far as their motives were concerned than what the network news reported.

WALTER CRONKITE, in my opinion, epitomizes the internationalist point of view that some elite media types embrace. Uncle Walter, who is still well respected around the country, made no secret of his loathing for how the Bush administration handled the Iraq War. So I filed this analysis, which was printed in hundreds of newspapers across the country:

> No surprise, ideologues on both the left and the right are screaming that the media coverage of the Iraq War is slanted away from their beliefs. The sound and the fury of the partisans is predictable and not very important, because there are so many media outlets that the sheer amount of information Americans can potentially get obliterates any narrow agenda an individual journalist might have.
>
> As far as TV news is concerned, the reportorial flow of information is occasionally tainted by a biased remark, but this is not a serious problem because, again, there is just so much verbiage. However, there is a philosophical divide among the broadcast anchor people and this you should know about.
>
> In a speech at Drew University last week, Walter Cronkite harshly criticized the war and the Bush administration, saying: "The arrogance of our spokespeople, even the president himself, has been exceptional and it seems to me they [other countries] have taken great umbrage at that. We have told them what they must do. It is a pretty dark doctrine."
>
> It seems to me that the 83-year-old former CBS anchor is

minimizing the fact that the Bush administration did try to work though the United Nations to disarm Iraq. And while it is true that many in the Bush administration could do with a Dale Carnegie seminar, it is also true that America was royally screwed in the UN Security Council by our so-called allies. Ask Colin Powell what he thinks of the way the French have conducted themselves.

But the real problem with Cronkite's analysis is that he looks at the situation from an international point of view, while the President and some other newsmen, including your humble correspondent, look at the Iraq conflict from an American perspective.

Walter Cronkite is an internationalist. That is, he sees other countries in the world as being on an equal footing with America when vital situations arise. A few other national TV anchormen are internationalists as well in varying degrees.

But there are major problems with covering the American war on terror from an internationalist point of view. As a journalist I want to be fair, but I also want President Bush to put the protection of Americans above the economic and political concerns of other countries. Call me a jingoist, but your family's security is more to me than Gerhard Schroeder's political career. I understand that some countries are angry that Mr. Bush rejected the Kyoto environmental agreement and, like Bill Clinton, I feel their pain. But not nearly as much as the pain I felt watching three thousand of my countrymen die on 9/11. So if some egomaniacal leader like Jacques Chirac is going to protect Saddam Hussein because he doesn't like Bush's style, I am going to knock Chirac. Hard.

But Uncle Walter doesn't see it that way. He sees the war on Iraq as "pre-emptive" and unnecessary because it doesn't have worldwide validation. Mr. Cronkite believes that the agendas of other countries should be considered when making decisions about the defense of Americans, even when those agendas are based on greed and petty politics. I strongly disagree.

The truth is that Walter Cronkite stood by and said little while the Vietnam War raged out of control in the 1960s. Finally, he confronted the lies and deceit the Johnson administration perpetrated on the American public, but Cronkite's conversion came very late in that deadly game.

When President Clinton bombed Milosevic's Belgrade, circumventing the United Nations and ignoring the objections of France and Russia, Cronkite said nothing publicly. Maybe he didn't notice the bombing was "pre-emptive" and that many nations disapproved.

So while Mr. Cronkite is an internationalist, he seems to be a selective one. But even if he were consistent in giving equal weight to the policies of other countries vis-à-vis the security of the U.S.A., he would be wrong.

American journalists commenting about the war on terror are obligated to inform their listeners or readers if they see the world as a level playing field. If Walter Cronkite believes that the French view of the terror threat is just as valid as the American view, then he needs to clearly state that so that people like me can challenge him.

Look at it this way. In covering World War II, the young Cronkite would have never given the Spanish view of the war the same weight as the American view. Franco's Spain was sympathetic to Hitler. As a responsible reporter, Cronkite could not have possibly done that.

Yet, in the war on terror, Cronkite and others like him want a "world consensus" on how to deal with villains like Saddam. That is truly misguided and might even be dangerous to the health of Americans. But Francisco Franco would love it.

That column angered some in the elite media. Tough. What I wrote was and is true. We have a bunch of very powerful people in the press who give moral equivalencies to foreign countries and even to organizations and philosophies that are bent on harming the U.S.A. That ecumenical view is simply awful.

One final word about Mr. Cronkite, who shortly after that controversy had to disengage himself from a medical product he was endorsing for money. It was an embarrassing episode, but I did not deal with it on *The Factor*. That's because I have nothing against the man and have no idea what happened in the commercial brouhaha, which also featured CBS's Morley Safer and Aaron Brown of CNN. My beef with Cronkite concerned a policy opinion he made public. I simply disagreed with it, and just because he's Walter Cronkite doesn't mean I can't call him out. People like to think that if you disagree with someone's opinion you are attacking *them*. That is just dumb. Cronkite is a broadcasting legend and deserves his status. But the ground he walks on is not sacred and he was wrong about the Iraq War. And perhaps the tongue-lashing was good for Uncle Walter. Two months later, he announced that he himself was going to write a syndicated newspaper column and outed himself as a "liberal." I was shocked, I tell you, just shocked!

My support for the removal of Saddam Hussein was based on logic and data. In the months leading up to the war, I simply tossed out emotion and examined the facts.

1. In 1991 Saddam Hussein invaded Kuwait but was forced out by a coalition led by the United States. In the process 293 Americans died in Desert Storm.

2. As part of the peace agreement that Saddam signed to end the First Gulf War, he agreed to give up all of his weapons of mass destruction (WMDs) and allow United Nations weapons inspectors to verify his compliance.

3. Saddam Hussein then proceeded to violate eighteen United Nations mandates to disarm and, in 1998, refused to allow the weapons inspectors any further access inside Iraq. Finally, more than four years later, at the urging of the United States, UN Resolution 1441 was passed demanding that Saddam produce his WMDs immediately or face "serious consequences."

4. After Saddam defied 1441, the United Nations refused to confront Saddam militarily. The reasons were primarily political and economic. As we now know, France, Russia, and Germany were making millions of dollars doing business, some of it illegal, with Saddam. The U.S.A. and Britain complained bitterly, but to no avail.

5. After September 11 the United States embarked on a world-

wide defensive strategy to hunt down terrorists and their enablers wherever a situation posed a perceived danger. Saddam was certainly a terrorist enabler, giving sanctuary to killers like Abu Nidal and Abu Abbas and training Hamas executioners. With his self-admitted stocks of anthrax and other impossible-to-detect chemical and biological weapons, the evil dictator was in a position to supply various terrorist groups with doomsday substances. You'll remember that just a few envelopes dipped in anthrax nearly shut down the U.S. government in the days after 9/11.

So, using logical thinking, I came to the conclusions that Saddam had violated the Gulf War treaty, was a potential danger to the U.S.A., could not be contained by Hans Blix and his crew of UN weapons inspectors, and was a psychopathic murderer who had to be confronted in order to prevent any further atrocities.

Before Al Qaeda hit us on 9/11, the U.S.A. could rationalize that allowing monsters like Saddam to remain in power could not be at the sole discretion of America. After all, the world is full of brutal dictators, and the U.S.A. is not mandated to remove them all from power. But with fanatical Muslims dedicated to using any and all methods in order to kill American civilians, it would have been irresponsible for an American president to allow the United Nations to permit Saddam, a man with a huge list of undetermined WMDs in his arsenal, to continue his rule. What did our people die for in 1991? If peace treaties are worth nothing, then this world will soon descend into chaos. I firmly believe that had Al Gore been elected in 2000, he would have done the same thing that President Bush did. Certainly his running mate, Senator Joseph Lieberman, fully supported the war against Iraq.

My support for the war drew the ire of publications like the *New York Times* and the *Los Angeles Times*, perhaps the most ideological of all the elite media. Both publications falsely accused me of being a political partisan because I felt the forced removal of Saddam was the right thing to do. Of course, my analysis of the situation had nothing to do with partisan politics. It had everything to do with justice and protecting the American people.

I have also stated on many occasions that I respect honest dissent. For that reason those who opposed the war on principle, and not from anti-Bush ideology, were given a fair hearing on *The Factor*. The actor Mike Farrell had eight minutes in which to put forth his point of view, and I challenged it. It was an illuminating debate, and in the end Mr. Farrell said that no matter what the outcome in Iraq, he would not admit President Bush was right. And, of course, it is Farrell's right to state that. However, it is a wise person who leaves some room for the possibility that he or she is wrong.

More than a few antiwar protestors used their opposition as the occasion to take partisan shots and promote a variety of other causes. Even worse, some antiwar protestors tried to take the high moral ground, which I found incredibly offensive. *All* sincerely held beliefs should be respected, especially when the issue of war had so many unanswered questions. The brutal truth is that the only people who possessed absolute moral certainty in this conflict were the ones who died for their country. The military heroes and heroines alone held the high moral ground, and nobody should forget it.

THE MORAL QUESTIONS surrounding the war became even thornier when Pope John Paul II weighed in by calling the conflict "unjust." The Pontiff, obviously a man of peace, openly objected to the coalition's invasion of Iraq. This is not meant as a cheap shot, but I wish the Pope had brought the same kind of moral passion to the priest pedophilia scandal we discussed earlier.

Anyway, in response to the Pope's position, I wrote this in March 2003:

It is fairly easy to understand why France, Germany, China, and Russia oppose removing Iraqi dictator Saddam Hussein by force. Those countries are doing profitable business with Saddam, and all of them would like to see American power diminished.

But Pope John Paul is another matter. His opposition to military action is understandable in theory but troubling in practice.

John Paul has sent his emissary, Pio Cardinal Laghi, to tell President Bush that attacking Iraq would be unjust and immoral. That's like sending Sister Mary Theresa to tell Eminem to stop cursing. The President is firmly convinced that Saddam is an evil man with murder on his mind. Short of Jesus appearing in the Oval Office with an opposing point of view, Bush is not going to change his opinion.

The Catholic Church embraces the tradition of "just war." That is, any use of force must be accompanied by clear and convincing evidence that only force will solve a situation that is both threatening and immoral. And since there is the possibility that UN weapons inspectors might be able to restrain Saddam, the Pope believes there are still options to war.

The problem with that argument is faith, pardon the pun. The Pope is putting his faith in a system of inspections that very well might fail. If that happens and even a portion of Saddam's unaccounted-for 8,500 liters of anthrax is used against people, a worldwide catastrophe would ensue.

The Pope does not answer questions, so it is impossible to know what he thinks about that possibility. We also don't know how John Paul squares keeping Saddam in power, considering his murderous past. It's one thing for the Vatican to condemn Saddam's gassing of the Kurds, mass murder and rape in Kuwait, and funding of suicide bombing expeditions—it is quite another to prevent those things.

So what are America's 65 million Catholics supposed to do? Theologically, the Pope is on firm ground. Humanistically, he is one of the many Saddam enablers. If the nations of the world would unite against evil things like Saddam, and the insanity of countries like North Korea, deadly situations would be solved and the world would be a better, safer place.

But the world will not unite against evil, and the Pope does not call for that practical unification. Instead, he calls for peace. Does he really believe Saddam and North Korea's Kim Jong Il are listening?

The Catholic Church teaches *tranquillitas ordinis,* the peace of order, which is supposed to be imposed by legal and political means. But as the world has seen, Osama Bin Laden, Adolf Hitler, and, yes, Saddam Hussein have not been bullish on the peace of order. Instead, they have embraced the practice of violent chaos.

As a loyal Catholic, I am glad the Pope is praying for America and for peace. I pray his prayers will work a miracle and Saddam will be removed from power without bloodshed.

But if that miracle is not forthcoming, this Catholic does not have faith that Saddam will not use his outlawed anthrax somewhere down the line.

And so, to prevent the mass death that took place in Europe and Asia while another Pope was praying sixty years ago, I support the moral quest of removing a dangerous killer from power. God forgive me.

Endorsing the war against Saddam did not mean I was "prowar," as the simpletons who want to demonize their policy opponents would have you believe. Up until the last moment, I believed (and was praying for) a possible scenario whereby the coward Saddam along with his two thug sons would abdicate. That would have been the best solution for the world.

I<small>T IS CERTAINLY</small> true that the Fox News Channel launched its war coverage with less skepticism than any of the other broadcast news services. Led by *The Factor*'s analysis, FNC wanted the

U.S.A. and its satellites to win the fight; there was never any question about that. While ABC News and others openly doubted the righteousness and practicality of the action, FNC thought the opposite—a viewpoint that was well within ethical editorial bounds. Our reporters, both embedded and otherwise, were told not to strike an editorial tone (and most did not), but FNC analysts did provide mostly pro-American opinion.

This approach brought vicious attacks on us by some who did not agree with that opinion. But it also brought record-high ratings led by *The Factor,* which soared into the top position among all cable news programs for the duration of the war. In other words, the 70 percent of the American people who believed the conflict was just were those who voted with their remote-control devices.

Predictably, that response drove our critics even crazier. Some of our competitors screamed that Fox and O'Reilly pandered to patriotism or carried water for the Bush administration. But the true reason we destroyed CNN and NBC in the cable ratings was obvious: We reported accurately and *we were right!*

On the eve of the invasion, the *New York Times* editorialized that the war was "reckless." The *Los Angeles Times* viewed it as a "disaster." In the first few days of the war, both newspapers slanted their headlines in an attempt to bolster their fallacious predictions. If you were reading either of those papers, you would have thought the coalition was actually losing the war. The situation was so egregious that I actually got mad at the pulp fiction that was in my hands. So, three days after the war began, I opened *The Factor* with a comparison of the front-page headlines in the *Boston Globe* and the *New York Times*. Both are owned by the same company but have editorial independence. The *Globe*'s headlines were accurate—the coalition was doing well and consolidating gains. The *Times*'s headlines were exactly the opposite. I'll tell you more about this shortly.

On television Peter Jennings, as mentioned, was openly skeptical about the war. Dan Rather and Tom Brokaw maintained their poker faces, but much of the copy they read was laced with doubt. Of course, most of the doubt evaporated three weeks later when Saddam's statue hit the pavement. It is my belief that the loss of credibility on the part of some major newspapers and broadcasters will be permanent.

During the second week of the war, as the U.S. infantry and the Marines were driving steadily toward Baghdad, Fox News military analyst David Hunt handed me an e-mail he had just received directly from the forward lines. It was written by an army lieutenant colonel who was moving his 3rd Infantry Division at an incredible pace. Here's the pithy part of the missive:

The plan is going exactly as scripted; the news reports are full of shit. We have control of central Iraq and our casualties are light. Just today we destroyed two divisions, and six other Iraqi divisions have decided not to fight. The news never reports this. We have probably killed close to 10,000. Every soldier is getting a chance to engage and kill the enemy. Iraq has these death squad guys, Fedayeen Saddam, and they continuously make suicidal charges at our tanks, brads, and checkpoints. We are happy to send them to hell. You would not believe the carnage. Imagine your street knee-deep with body parts, with hundreds of vehicles burning, including the occupants. We fill up trucks with body parts daily. . . .

I knew this letter was accurate and therefore also knew that many of the mainstream media reports were inaccurate. The carnage they were reporting simply did not stack up against actual coalition casualties. American and British killed-in-action (KIA) stats were extremely low, while the *New York Times* and others were reporting "widespread fierce resistance." The *Los Angeles Times* was just as misleading, so I decided to call the papers on their coverage. Thank God I was right.

The knockout punch to the *New York Times* was delivered shortly after the war began. As I mentioned, I opened *The Factor* with a look at the front pages of the *Boston Globe* and the *Times*. Both papers have liberal editorial pages. But the *Globe*'s page-one headlines suggested a war that was going fairly well in its early stages, *while every single headline the* New York Times *placed on page one was negative for the coalition*. I asked what the hell was going on.

The reaction to the comparison of the two papers was thunderous. Thousands of Americans e-mailed the *Times* with harsh complaints, and copied those missives to me at *The Factor*. Thousands of others called my radio talk show, voicing bitter condemnation. The *Times* could not deny what its headline writers had wrought. The next day the tone of the headlines changed dramatically: Only half of the headlines skewed negative.

It may have been a pyrrhic victory, however. No question I severely embarrassed the *New York Times* and also the *Los Angeles Times,* which, during the three weeks of fighting in Iraq, ran some of the most irresponsible op-ed pieces I have ever seen. But of course there will be reprisals because the elite media does not tolerate being held accountable. They will come after me.

But I had to expose the situation. There simply wasn't a choice if I wanted to remain true to the No Spin Zone philosophy. Many in the elite media were not looking out for you by inaccurately reporting what was happening in the beginning stages of the war. The headline writers and some editors were editing and slanting copy to suit their editorial feelings. This is terribly dishonest and makes me sick. So I busted them. This may sound self-congratulatory to you. If so, I'm sorry. My intent is not to put myself up as a hero. It is to report accurately what happened during the media war at home.

THROUGHOUT THE IRAQ conflict my analysis was mostly correct, but I did make a few mistakes: I bought the weapons of mass destruction argument too quickly and failed to predict how politicized the war would be. I should have known that the Bush administration would have to fight with one hand tied behind its back in consideration of public opinion. For that reason the U.S. military did not utilize most of its vast power. The only thing that shocked and awed me was the misreporting I saw.

In hindsight, the Pentagon's cautious strategy was understandable. The more dead Arabs lying in the sand and streets of Iraq, the greater the anger the Muslim world would feel against the U.S.A. You will never hear the Defense Department confirm the actual total of dead Iraqi soldiers. All KIA stats will probably be classified. Truth be told, with *real* shock and awe, the war in Iraq could have been won in less than a week. But give the Bush administration credit: The victory was enormous, coalition casualities were fewer than 150 dead, and a brutal dictator got what he deserved.

The euphoria of the victory wore off quickly, however, when the weapons of mass destruction chaos kicked in. In the months after Saddam was removed, only a couple of mobile labs were found and, as you know, the antiwar crowd kicked into high gear with the "Bush lied about WMDs" chant. The truth about the matter is this: Mr. Bush wanted to remove Saddam, and his intelligence chieftains played to that sentiment. People like CIA director George Tenet felt confident that because Saddam would not account for the biological weapons the United Nations inspectors said he possessed, there must be something he didn't want the world to know. This is logical thinking and, indeed, both Bill Clinton and Al Gore, as well as every congressperson on the intelligence committee, bought into that thinking.

Seeking presidential approval, the intelligence agencies then dumped critical thinking and set out to prove the WMD threat. And they did come up with circumstantial evidence, supplying the Bush administration with photos and tape recordings that apparently indicated the Iraqis were hiding WMDs. That's the stuff Secretary of State Colin Powell used at his UN briefing in

February 2003. The American public, jittery after 9/11, bought the perceived danger and the game was on.

It is fair to say that President Bush wanted to neutralize Saddam and found a way to make it happen. It is also fair to say that if Saddam had allowed the UN inspectors full access, he might still be executing people today. Saddam defied UN mandates for years, and Bush finally called him on it. If you put ideology aside, you can see the logic of the situation. The Bush administration felt Saddam was destabilizing the Middle East and thumbing his nose at the United Nations. If that situation were allowed to go unchallenged, the Middle East would never calm down, and other rogue nations would also defy the United Nations. I believe that Mr. Bush and British Prime Minister Tony Blair convinced themselves there *had* to be weapons of mass destruction under Saddam's control. Why else would he continue his foolish defiance? In the end, the world is a better place because Saddam was ousted, but the Bush haters and conspiracy people have yet another scenario to keep them happy.

FINALLY, SOME IN the press really did look out for you. The embedded correspondents from all papers and TV networks generally reported the truth with courage and vibrance. There was a minimum of bad reporting. I was amazed at how good the information flow was, and I saw just about everything on television while reading dozens of newspapers and newsmagazines. These men and women in the Iraq killing field were truly magnificent. It was the ideologically blinded editors, safely ensconced back home, who performed villainous acts. One BBC correspondent actually made public a letter he sent to his London superiors demanding that they stop slanting his coverage. The reporters in the field were heroes, while the editors in the newsrooms, at least some of them, were the cowards.

And no, I'm not forgetting Peter Arnett. He was not an embedded reporter. He was a Baghdad guy. Arnett is a brave man, but he lost it. Saying on Iraqi TV that the coalition war plan had failed was not only stupidly wrong, it gave Saddam's killers hope and could have possibly lengthened the war. Fighters without hope usually surrender or disappear. Fighters with hope kill people. Arnett is truly the poster boy for the Stockholm Syndrome because he actually began identifying with his Baghdad handlers. I feel sorry for Peter. I wish things had turned out differently for him. I really do.

At the same time, it gave me no joy to see people like Janeane Garofalo, Sean Penn, Mike Farrell, Susan Sarandon, Tim Robbins, Martin Sheen, et al., humiliated by their "Chicken Little" opposition to the forced removal of Saddam. As I mentioned, sincere dissent should always be respected. But if you put yourself out there and you make a mistake, admit it. Don't do what the Dixie Chicks did. Don't speak provocatively about a subject you don't know much about and then claim, "Well, I have the freedom to say what I want."

That's true, but that's stupid. Natalie Maines is not going for her Ph.D. in political science anytime soon. The Chicks' lead singer does have a right to spout off about any subject, no question. But if she offends millions by insulting the President during wartime, and then can't explain the origins of her dissatisfaction about the war (as she couldn't when Diane Sawyer interviewed her), she is going to look foolish and perhaps venal. The result will be that some fans will no longer support her commercial enterprises. That's life in the controversial lane.

Remember, the Constitution gives you the right to be a moron. And millions of us exercise that right all the time. But sometimes there is a price to be paid.

Finally, the war in Iraq proves once again that ideologues can never look out for you. They are too blinded by the light on the right or the left and they will never see things for what they really are. If you become an ideological prisoner, the truth will always elude you because you will never seek it. Instead, you'll evaluate each issue and problem with an agenda: trying to prove your ideology is correct.

The antidote to this is to reject a rigid political philosophy and discipline yourself to think logically. Gather facts. Facts always look out for you. And that's a fact.

CHAPTER SEVEN

You Have the Right to Remain Silent

I shot the sheriff, but I did not shoot the deputy.

—*Bob Marley, "I Shot the Sheriff"*

THERE IS A simple reason that the average American lawyer makes nearly $90,000 a year, and that is because any kind of legal situation will cost you dearly, both financially and emotionally. Once again, here is the blunt truth: The so-called "justice system" in America is not looking out for you, and you should write that down and read it every day of your life. If you are poor and you are arrested, things will get very bad, very soon. If you have money, justice might come around a bit quicker, but you will find yourself writing enormous checks on a regular basis. Lawyers charge by the hour, and at $400 per, just saying "Hi there, Perry Mason" to one will cost you ten bucks.

Generally speaking, however, any kind of legal problem is going to remove assets from your possession. So think very hard before misbehaving or suing somebody for throwing trash on your lawn. Even the contingency crowd (lawyers who charge only if they win a settlement) may peck you to death with "expenses." The American justice system is a runaway money train where those without legal credentials are tied to the tracks.

The reality is that judges and lawyers and cops and everybody else in the law business belong to a club. And that club wants you to pay the dues but not become a member. Deals are made all the time in the club. Lawyers and judges often know each other, have "relationships," and, for one reason or another, have a vested interest in seeing the club prosper. You, the U.S. citizen, are just passing through the club and will not even be offered valet parking.

And the club is doing very, very well. From 1984 to 1999, criminal cases rose 47 percent and civil cases 32 percent in state courts across the country, according to the National Center for Tort Reform. Everybody involved in the legal system is making money except those whom the system is supposedly designed to protect. No matter how you get involved in the legal system, you will pay. Trust me on this.

Since I can't stand the unfairness of the legal world and even get stomachaches writing about it, this chapter will be very short. But I want to give you a vivid example of how corrupt the American legal system has become, and how it most definitely does not look out for you or for any other nonmember.

REMEMBER THE brutal murder of seven-year-old Danielle van Dam in San Diego? She was snatched out of her house while her parents were smoking pot and her father was fooling around with one of his wife's friends (the couple had a self-admitted "open marriage"). Anyway, little Danielle was brutally raped and murdered and buried in a desert.

Immediately under suspicion in the case was a neighbor of the van Dams, a middle-aged guy named David Westerfield. The man was a perverted creep. Child pornography was found on computer disks in his office. Almost at once, the cops knew he did it, but Danielle's body could not be found, making a provable case very difficult. The police, however, did have evidence that Danielle had been in Westerfield's presence. The little girl's hair, blood, and fingerprints were found in Westerfield's motor home. Other hairs from Danielle were found on his bed.

As the evidence mounted against Westerfield, his attorneys, Steven Feldman and Robert Boyce, began actively negotiating a plea bargain with authorities. The *San Diego Union-Tribune* reported the situation: "Minutes before Danielle van Dam's remains were found on Feb. 27, David Westerfield's lawyers were brokering a deal with prosecutors. He would tell police where he dumped the 7-year-old girl's body; they would not seek the death penalty. . . . Prosecutors were seriously considering the bargain when Danielle's body was discovered. . . . The 'deal was just minutes away,' one of the sources said." But after the body was discovered, the lawyers "no longer 'had anything to discuss regarding a plea bargain.'"

And so the case went to trial but, by law, any discussions of the plea deal were not admissible in court. Even the judge was not aware of the proposed plea bargain. But Westerfield's lawyers obviously knew their client was guilty, because they *offered the location of the body*! Nevertheless, during the trial Feldman and Boyce mounted a defense based partly on the unprovable and completely immoral theory that acquaintances of the van Dams, who were in the house on the night the girl disappeared, could have been the killers. In the process, these defense lawyers destroyed the reputations of the van Dams, who were still grieving for their little daughter, and their acquaintances. Unbelievable.

The only active participants in any criminal trial who are not under oath are the attorneys and the judge. So the attorneys can say just about anything they want to say. But there are rules against lying or intentionally misleading the jury, and they are supposed to be enforced. I said they are *supposed* to be.

In reality there is little enforcement against unethical conduct by defense attorneys. As we will show in a moment, Feldman and Boyce knowingly misled the jury and got away with it. But their client, thank God, did not. Despite the actions of Westerfield's lawyers, he was convicted by a jury and sentenced to death. The physical evidence presented by the prosecution was overwhelming and finally did the killer in. He is still on death row, awaiting execution. But after the trial I told some of the jurors about the proposed deal Feldman and Boyce had reportedly offered. They were stunned. One juror, Raymond Winkowski, said that he could not believe the lawyers had attempted to mislead the jury and, in the process, smeared the reputations of the van Dams.

On September 18, 2002, I interviewed Mr. Winkowski on *The Factor*.

O'REILLY: Now, when you were listening to Feldman paint a scenario that Danielle van Dam's parents might have been responsible for her death by allowing strangers to come into the home, the lawyer was believable, wasn't he?

WINKOWSKI: Oh, yeah. He was very believable.

O'REILLY: And the jury took his scenarios seriously?

WINKOWSKI: Oh yes. He impressed us a lot.

O'REILLY: But now that you find out that Feldman made it all up, that he knew his client was guilty because, according to the Tribune, he offered a deal, what do you think?

WINKOWSKI: I don't see how anyone could do that. I really do not.

Rule 5200 of the California Bar Rules of Conduct states: "A lawyer shall not seek to mislead the judge, judicial officer, or jury by an artifice or false statement of fact or law." An "artifice" means a fabricated action or account.

In my opinion, Feldman and Boyce clearly violated Rule 5200. But did the California Bar do anything about it? No, it did not. After the interview with Raymond Winkowski aired, *The Factor* and hundreds of our viewers filed complaints against the two attorneys. The California Bar was inundated.

And so was I, as hundreds of letters from attorneys around the country arrived chastising me for my criticism. San Diego criminal defense attorney William Nimmo came on *The Factor* and said this to me: "I don't think you understand what the duty of a defense lawyer is. . . . Our job, regardless of what we know, regardless of what our client knows, is to put on a vigorous defense, which means cross-examining witnesses even we know are truth-ful, putting up scenarios that we know might even not be correct."

In other words, counselor Nimmo is saying any kind of fabrica-tion is fine as long as it is used in a "vigorous defense." I chal-lenged him on it, asking: "Are you denying they lied?"

"I'm not denying that they maybe put up a defense that they didn't believe in," Nimmo shot back.

"They lied, counselor," I said.

"That's their duty and their obligation."

Are you shocked by Nimmo's stance? If so, you must have missed the O. J. Simpson trial. Anything goes in court these days, and the cleverest, not the most honest, lawyers usually win. This is justice? This is "the whole truth and nothing but the truth"? If the witnesses, investigators, and defendants have to tell the truth, you are telling me the lawyers don't? That is exactly what the jus-tice system is saying, and the result is that killers, rapists, dope dealers, and other dangerous individuals are put right back out on the streets even as the lawyers cash their checks.

Luckily for society, but no thanks to his devious lawyers, David Westerfield will get what he deserves, but little solace can be taken from that, because if his lawyers had been successful with their sleazy ruse, a child killer would have escaped the death penalty. It has happened before.

On February, 19, 2003, *The Factor* received a letter from the chief trial counsel of the State Bar of California, Mike Nisperos, Jr., which said in part: "After reviewing the relevant portions of the [court] transcript, we determined that the conduct of Mr. Feldman and Mr. Boyce was within the scope of historical and ethical parameters of practice by a criminal defense attorney. In the opinion of the trial court, the trial District Attorney and this office, there is no basis to support any charge of misconduct."

One problem with the contents of that letter: The San Diego district attorney who prosecuted Westerfied, Paul Pfingst, came on *The Factor* and said no one at the California Bar had ever contacted him, and had someone done so, he would have told them that the conduct of Feldman and Boyce violated a number of ethical canons. The Bar covered up for Westerfield's lawyers. We immediately refiled the complaint.

But I don't expect any satisfaction here. The club almost always sticks together. The fact that Mr. Pfingst came forward publicly is very unusual. He will probably lose his club privileges for a while.

Let's sum up the prosecution's case in this matter: The defense attorneys for child killer David Westerfield were cleared of any and all wrongdoing even though they knowingly fabricated a scenario to try to get this monster set free. And that's the truth, the whole truth, and nothing but the truth. So help me God.

OUR JUSTICE SYSTEM is overburdened, driven by money and connections, and sometimes downright corrupt, and few in power seem to care. *The Factor* was the only news organization that condemned Feldman and Boyce, who are not alone in their actions. Where was the rest of the media? This is a disgraceful situation and one that should be addressed by the Supreme Court immediately.

But it won't be, because the Supreme Court justices are not proactive. They are like lizards sunning on a rock. They don't move unless something comes along. The lawyer lobby in this country is too rich and too powerful. Too much money is made every day from legal sleight-of-hand and outright deception for any meaningful reform to take place. Ask any police officer what he or she thinks of defense techniques in general. All of them will tell you horror stories.

Americans like to think that our country is a place where all citizens can get a "fair" trial before a jury of our peers. But if lawyers are allowed to deceive, fabricate, smear, and intimidate without consequence, where is the fairness? Our criminal justice system has become a farce where high-priced lawyers armed with vivid imaginations run wild. And the civil courts are even worse, with many cases taking years even to be heard while legal expenses mount astronomically.

So, if you possibly can, stay away from all this. It is a cesspool of corruption; even if you win you'll get hurt. I love this country, but I despise what our so-called system of justice has degenerated into. If you're an unscrupulous lawyer, the system looks out for you. If you are looking for an honest day in court, well, you have my sympathy, because you are not likely to get it.

CHAPTER EIGHT

Minority Report

Why do I find it hard to write the next line?
Oh, I want the truth to be said.

—*Spandau Ballet, "True"*

I KNOW THIS MUCH to be true: It is not easy being a minority in the United States. Not only are you outnumbered, but the crushing weight of irrational ignorance is, generally speaking, directed toward you far more than it is at the majority. Sometimes whites in the U.S.A. overlook racial bias entirely because it does not affect them.

For example, I recently reported the story of an all-white high school prom that was being held in rural Georgia. It was obviously exclusionary but also totally unnecessary. Taylor County High, a school that is equally divided between blacks and whites, had scheduled a prom for everybody, so there was no apparent need for the segregated version. And nobody put forth a good reason for holding it. I blasted the prom, figuring that after 9/11 and the Iraq

War, where about 20 percent of the casualties were African-American, there would be a huge outrage against this kind of insult. I was wrong.

Instead of condemnation, I heard a litany of excuses from school officials and talk show bloviators. The Republican governor of Georgia, Sonny Perdue, ran for cover, refusing to issue direct statements about the event. Perdue actually sent his black press secretary to confront me on *The Factor*, where, predictably, she got hammered in the debate after she claimed that the governor was too busy to address the issue.

And that wasn't hard to do, because an all-white high school dance is indefensible in a country named the *United* States. I told the governor's press lady that the prom was hurtful to the black students attending Taylor High and that Perdue had a leadership obligation to scorn the event. But he would not.

So it is undeniable that white leadership on racial questions is often lacking. But so, too, is black leadership. Jesse Jackson and Al Sharpton were nowhere to be found during the prom controversy, and the black legislators on Capitol Hill were also missing in action. Maybe they don't consider an incident like this important. But they are also mostly silent on black crime, horrendous rap lyrics, and the disintegration of the African-American family.

It doesn't take John Shaft to figure out there is a lack of national leadership in the minority community because, inexplicably, the big picture eludes many so-called minority spokespeople. And more than a few national minority leaders are really demagogues who feed their followers lies and deceptions in order to accumulate money and power.

I'm sometimes asked why I do so much reporting and analysis of minority issues, and my reply is brief: because few others do and all Americans deserve equal justice and a fair chance at the pursuit of happiness. The elite media are literally scared speechless of offending minorities in America and thus shy away from most confrontational reporting on situations that injure those who do not have the resources to fight effectively for themselves. For all of the politically correct rhetoric you hear or read in the press, little is actually being done to right wrongs on the tough side of town.

CHANCES ARE THAT you have never heard of the Englewood neighborhood on the infamous South Side of Chicago unless you're a jazz fan. During Chicago's jazz age, the area was vibrant and safe, but now it is a terrifying place for the people who live there, marked by vacant lots and boarded-up storefronts that, at night, house dangerous people. In the last ten years, about seven hundred people have been murdered in this area, which spans just four square miles and has a population of one hundred thousand mostly poor and working-class people.

The problem in Englewood is a drug gang called the Gangster Disciples. They kill and terrorize law-abiding Americans to protect their lucrative turf. Authorities estimate the gang reaps about $1 million *a week* from selling narcotics. The gang employs hundreds of residents, mostly teenagers, to move the poison and watch for police. The action is round-the-clock and never ends.

Of course, the Chicago authorities know this, and so do the federal drug agencies. But the situation is allowed to exist.

The same scenario would not be acceptable in Malibu, in Georgetown, in the Hamptons, or on Park Avenue. Drug gangs would not be permitted to stand in front of million-dollar houses, selling illegal substances. Many cops would arrive and forcibly remove said dealers if they ever tried it, which they wouldn't. But on the South Side of Chicago and in thousands of other similar neighborhoods across the U.S.A., the brutal hoods can do pretty much what they want. That is *not* equal justice under the law.

Some believe that skin color is the reason that the authorities allow inner-city chaos. But that is not the reason. As I wrote in my book *The O'Reilly Factor*, this is about class, not race. While racial bigots do exist, they are far less influential and effective than they used to be in America. Racism is death in corporate America, in law enforcement, in the media, in the military, in politics, and in every other powerful institution in the U.S.A. You simply cannot hold significant power in this country if you are out to hurt or are even insensitive to a specific racial or religious group. If you don't believe me, ask Trent Lott.

No, it's not racism but cowardice that allows evil dope pushers to run wild in the Englewoods of the country. Few in power want to confront the problem, because there is little gain in it for them. Unfortunately, many powerful people in America will do the right thing only if it will directly benefit themselves. Cleaning up drug trafficking in poor neighborhoods does not win elections, lead to high lecture fees, or excite public adulation. The street drug life is a tough, ingrained, unpleasant situation with racial overtones all day long. Few in power want to go near it; that's why there's no solution in sight.

So, while overt racism is not the primary reason inner-city neighborhoods are neglected and overlooked, *stealth* racism is definitely in play in America. That is sneaky bigotry that, sometimes unintentionally, insults and demeans. Those who justified the prom situation are good examples of Americans embracing stealth racism, at least on that issue. Fortunately, stealth racism is mostly petty in its application. But it is hurtful nonetheless to anyone who experiences it.

HOWEVER, **HERE IS** truth number one if you are a minority American looking for a full shot at the pursuit of happiness: DON'T SWEAT THE SMALL STUFF. Ignorant behavior on the part of others often means nothing to your life. Overlook the insult, avoid the practitioner, and concentrate on doing constructive things that will make you a good person and a success in the workplace. I know it is easy for a guy like me to write that. I am not in your shoes. But it is solid advice.

But what exactly is "small stuff"? Well, here's an example. A very successful black female broadcaster has been a friend of mine for some time now. Recently, she was shopping in an upscale store, looking for luggage. She noticed a salesclerk watching her very closely. Of course, she was annoyed. Then the clerk came over and my friend asked to see a certain piece. She replied, "Oh, you know, that's very expensive."

Offensive? Sure. Racist? Possibly. Important? No. My friend just looked at the woman, rolled her eyes, and left the store. But the incident did upset her. I told her that was understandable but not worth her time. Dumb people are dumb people. You have a choice: Ignore them or confront them. In this case a cold stare was all the emotional wattage that person warranted.

But let's go back to Englewood for a moment. Cops and prosecutors know that it's impossible to enforce the law in any neighborhood if there is not cooperation between the people who live there and the authorities. In rich neighborhoods, most people love the police. They wave at them and smile and give them Christmas presents.

All is fine between the police and the citizenry.

Not so in the ghettos. Suspicion and animosity exist between the police and many poor people, and each side has valid reasons for the distrust. The cops know they are disliked, and they know the streets are dangerous. The folks know the police are sometimes resentful of the danger and hostility they face—and that resentment sometimes spills over into unpleasant confrontations, even with law-abiding citizens. Fear is present on both sides. And fear will always cause hostility.

In the 1930s my grandfather patrolled some tough poor neighborhoods in Brooklyn, New York, and had some very unkind things to say about lawbreakers and those who enabled them. But my "pop," as we called him, was willing to give up his life to protect an American of any color. He was no intellectual, but he was brave and honest. He could also be brutal and, at times, meted out street justice when he knew the guilty party would skate around the system and avoid punishment. My grandfather and his peers kept crime in the poor neighborhoods down by using a kind of low-grade vigilantism. Drug dealers were treated so harshly that they rarely appeared on my grandfather's beat for fear of him. Morphine addicts and street winos were also told to "move on." That's what they did if they wanted to avoid a measured dose of pain.

The result was that in these working-class and poor Brooklyn neighborhoods, children could play unsupervised in the streets and women could walk, with little fear, to the markets and movies after dark. Those were the Depression days, and nobody had much money. But everybody had the freedom to live and work in a protected environment. My grandfather took it personally if anyone on his beat got either assaulted physically or taken by a hustler. His network of informers would almost always pinpoint the guilty party. Pop and his coworkers took it from there. The word spread fast: Don't play illegal games in Flatbush.

That kind of "community policing" rarely happens today, which is probably a good thing. My grandfather had too much power and too little supervision. He was a good man, but some of his cohorts were not. Corruption and shakedowns were common, and so was racial invective. Fascism always causes crime to fall, but the consequences are always frightening. Absolute power corrupts absolutely. The brutalizers can produce order, but they almost always produce terror as well. Mussolini made the trains run on time in Italy, but his brown-shirted gang also could beat you to death for a misdemeanor.

There is, however, a middle ground. The residents of Englewood and other crime-ridden neighborhoods will never rid themselves of degenerates until they decide to cooperate with the system, however flawed it may be. Antipolice minority "leaders" are not looking out for the folks, they are hurting the folks. No one can confront criminals effectively but the police. They are the only ones with the power to remove pernicious people from the sidewalk in front of your home. Hating the cops is not going to help you. Is this understood? It is self-defeating. It is unfair and dangerous to your children.

THE COMMONSENSE RESPONSE to a crime siege, whether you're a minority or not, is to deal with the police through the churches. Dropping a dime on a drug dealer is dangerous, but speaking privately to your minister or priest about threatening situations is usually safe. Every poor neighborhood in the U.S.A. should have a church council, a group of local clergy that meets police liaisons on a weekly basis. At these private meetings information would be passed along, dangerous situations discussed. Clergy of all religions must take it upon themselves to stand up for fearful Americans who need help.

So why isn't this being done on a widespread basis all across the U.S.A.? Why haven't we heard Jesse Jackson or Al Sharpton or the rap stars or La Raza or any of the other powerful minority voices propose this? Because the church police solution is exactly that—a solution. And demagogues don't want solutions, at least ones for which they cannot take credit. No, many of the powerful minority lobbyists want to stoke up the hate, keep the racial divisions going. This is their strategy to gain and hold power. News flash: It works.

The racial demagogues have figured out that if there is no dragon (pressing problem, outrageous controversy), a white (or black) knight is not needed. And these demagogues want to control the dragon-slaying agenda. They don't want racial problem solving done by others, because that dilutes their power. As a result, a very few minority spokespeople push narrow, selfish agendas to the apathetic national media, which grants access to very few minorities. Thus, important work like protecting the good people of Englewood goes undone because there is no high-profile pressure to get anything changed.

There is, of course, hope. Many local leaders in besieged neighborhoods are trying to improve things. But for real change to happen in chaotic neighborhoods, there must be rules, strict rules. There must be a code of conduct that is widely accepted in the inner cities, just as there is in the affluent suburbs. Here is a creed that might be a place to start:

Having a child out of wedlock would be considered a harmful thing, something to discourage.

Drug selling would be considered a violent crime, and those involved in this most harmful of enterprises would be shunned and reported to the authorities though the churches.

Drug addiction and alcoholism would be considered contagious diseases. Those afflicted would be encouraged to get help but not looked upon as victims.

All kinds of child abuse and neglect would be confronted by the community immediately and reported to the proper authorities. There would be zero tolerance for adults who hurt or endanger kids.

Police would be assigned to provide protection at all public schools and would be stationed on campus to deal with disruptive and destructive students.

Curfews on teenagers would be enacted and enforced by local communities.

Zoning laws would be toughened and standards of care imposed on properties both public and private. Run-down buildings would be more easily condemned and then sold at auction to responsible builders.

Public nuisance laws would be passed so that individuals who disrespect neighborhoods and properties by actions such as graffiti, public lewdness and intoxication, incivility in words or deeds, littering, or the general creation of mayhem could be arrested and prosecuted by local authorities.

If that kind of creed was encouraged in all poor neighborhoods, and a cooperative discipline imposed by responsible citizens (who are the majority in every neighborhood), you would see the ghettos of the country gradually transformed into solid working-class enclaves. But no such creed has been proposed by the minority national leadership. Without the kind of mass exposure and pressure those people can bring, things are likely to get worse in chaotic districts.

And that's good if you are a racial hustler who has accumulated power by blaming the white man for everything. The more devastation you can point to in the minority communities, the more disciples you can sign up. A prosperous population has no need of divisive demagogues. A desperate population is vulnerable to exploitation by them.

WITHOUT A DOUBT, the number one problem among minority Americans is the collapse of the family. As I mentioned in Chapter Five, the rise in the percentage of children born out of wedlock has corresponded with the rise of secularism in America. There is no question about that. As late as the 1970s, there was a certain stigma imposed by society on a woman who got pregnant outside of marriage. No longer. Now it's "baby on board," and if no father is around to support it, hey, it's none of our business. The hell it isn't. The epidemic of out-of-wedlock kids is the primary source of poverty and social problems in this country. We all pay for that.

The statistics are brutal. As pointed out in Chapter Two, nearly 69 percent of African-American babies are now born to single mothers. For black women ages fifteen to twenty-four, that figure is an astounding 89 percent! That is simply a cultural collapse on an unprecedented scale for a developed country. Just the fact that nearly all black girls and young women having babies today are unmarried is enough to ensure social chaos within the African-American community for generations to come. A child without a secure support system will most likely be unable to compete with a child who has one. Thus the cycle of hopelessness and deprivation will continue.

So let me ask you this question. When was the last time you heard Jesse Jackson or Al Sharpton or even Colin Powell address this issue? When was the last time the elite media pointed it out to you? When was the last time there was a rally in Washington demanding that this colossal problem be addressed by all Americans?

Think about it. Trent Lott's foolish comments on race and segregation drew a thousand times more attention than the virtual collapse of the family infrastructure in the African-American community. And there is a definite reason for that.

Are you ready for some tough truth? Here it comes. The true reason minority problems are not effectively dealt with in the mass media and among powerful politicians is that the racial witch-hunters have hijacked all serious public policy debate by instilling a chilling fear into the national discourse. One dubious slip of the tongue can destroy a career, and all of us in the spotlight know it.

Racial witch-hunters are people who devote their lives to finding offense and then labeling the offender a "racist." There are also ethnic, religious, and sexual witch-hunters, all of whom do exactly the same thing with only the adjectives changing. Make one comment that can be construed as antiminority, and the witch-hunters fire up their torches and launch their mission to destroy your reputation. If you don't believe me, ask Mr. Lott, Senator Rick Santorum, Dr. Laura, Pat Buchanan, and dozens of other public figures who have run afoul of the politically correct demonizers.

Here's how the witch-hunting process works, and the simplicity of it would make the seventeenth-century Salem murderers smile. First a report surfaces, often in a gossip column, that some well-known person said something untoward. Many gossip columnists operate on the fringe of journalism, using anonymous sources and innuendo to fill their columns with titillating items designed to prick the famous. Liz Smith is an exception, but the American gossip industry is generally ruthlessly irresponsible and protected by libel laws so loose, they give a public person little if any recourse.

After the gossip item is published, the special-interest websites pick it up. Anger and angst are then generated among their readers, many of whom revel in this kind of stuff and could not care less about the truth. The Internet crowd blasts the libel all over the chat rooms, and bingo, it surfaces as "fact" in mainstream national publications.

The tragedy is that far too many minority Americans buy into this spectacle and enjoy the witch burning that results. The downside is that problems go unsolved and unaddressed. In our supersensitive society, offense is taken so easily that honest discussion of most controversial issues is virtually nonexistent, especially in the hallways of power. If there is absolutely any chance that a point of view can be twisted into a supposed ethnic insult, that point of view will not be uttered. This is why the Mexican border situation has been allowed to rage out of control and also why crime in the inner cities remains rampant. The powerful people who could tackle serious problems often pass on any subject that might possibly catch the eyes of the witch-hunters.

I **KNOW THIS** from personal experience. You may remember that I attacked the gangsta rap industry, including the rantings of white rapper Eminem, for selling mind poison to impressionable kids. The rappers couldn't win the debate because much of their stuff is so antisocial it's impossible to defend, so they tried to hang a racist tag on me. It didn't work, because most black Americans realize this garbage is destructive and hateful. But the witch-hunters tried.

That battle was noticed by the press. In April 2003 a witch-hunting ploy was manufactured by a vicious gossip writer in the *Washington Post*. *The Factor* had just come off a huge win with its coverage of the war, and some in the elite media were bitter and ready to rumble, especially because, as I mentioned earlier, I had embarrassed some print journalists.

For years I have been supporting a charity called The Best

Friends Foundation, a mentoring group that helps poor black kids around the country by matching them up with professional Americans who provide guidance and emotional support on a one-on-one basis. I believe this program and others like it are the keys to leveling the playing field somewhat for children who do not have strong support systems at home.

On Saturday, April 12, 2003, I emceed the annual Best Friends fund-raiser at the Marriott Wardman Park Hotel in Washington, D.C. There were more than seven hundred people in the ballroom, and close to a million dollars was raised. The theme was a sock hop, a sixties-type rock show featuring the Supremes, Bobby Vee, and Paul Revere and the Raiders. As part of my duties, I was asked to introduce some kids who would sing and dance before the professional performers came on. One of the groups was called the Ironmen, a bunch of boys in their early teens. One problem: The Ironmen weren't ready when they were summoned to the stage. So I went into a riff to kill time until they showed up. I used my Bill Murray voice, and this is exactly what I said:

"Where are the Ironmen? Are they in the Ironman bathroom? If so, get out here, you guys. Jeez, I hope they aren't out in the parking lot stealing hubcaps [an ironic throwback reference, as hubcap filching was big in the *American Graffiti* days]. Bring on the Ironmen!"

Suddenly, they came running out to amused, enthusiastic applause and did their number.

I know the evening was a great success, because everybody I encountered had a good time. I felt good about the whole deal.

Two days later that all changed.

Lloyd Grove, a gossip columnist for the *Washington Post,* is, in my opinion, a despicable human being. He makes his living hurting people and seems to have it in for the Fox News Channel. In the spring of 2003, Grove had to retract an item he wrote about Roger Ailes, the boss of Fox News. In that item Grove called Ailes an "adviser" to President Bush, knowing that such a label would ruin Roger's reputation for objectivity. Grove's boss got a missive from the Fox legal department, and the next day he retracted the item, saying he had "gone too far."

But before that episode, Grove zeroed in on me and wrote that I had made a "racially insensitive remark" at the Best Friends benefit. Apparently, Grove called Elayne Bennett, the president of Best Friends, asking about the hubcap remark.

Ms. Bennett told Grove that absolutely nothing offensive took place and the evening was a smashing success. She then called me and detailed what was going on. I was stunned. I called Grove and told him the whole thing was ridiculous. The next day he wrote this in the *Washington Post*:

THE UNFUNNY FACTOR

Maybe Bill O'Reilly should declare a "No-Quip Zone." Emceeing Saturday night's Best Friends rock-and-roll gala . . . the Fox News Channel star was trying to fill dead air during a lull in the entertainment. . . . O'Reilly ad-libbed: "Does anyone know where the Best Men [Ironmen] are? I hope they're not out in the parking lot stealing hubcaps."

"To say that this conservative audience—dominated by many

of Mr. O'Reilly's biggest fans—was aghast is an understatement," one attendee e-mailed us—asking for anonymity. "The well-known Republican politicians and their spouses seated *at* or near my table were appalled."

Oh, yeah? Then why couldn't Grove get one person to go on the record? Remember, there were more than seven hundred people in the room, many of whom were black. No one complained to me or to any member of the Best Friends board. In fact, no one even knew what Grove was referring to until more than forty-eight hours after the event. And why would anyone need anonymity? If I had done something offensive, wouldn't somebody have been outraged enough to step up? Who am I, Don Corleone?

In reply to that vicious column, Elayne Bennett issued this statement: "Bill O'Reilly has generously supported the Best Friends Foundation—specifically, our Best Men program for boys. He wrote a check that sent Best Men boys to summer camp. He made an offhand comment that was a New York Fonzie-style throwaway line. . . . We were very grateful that Bill O'Reilly took time from his family to donate his services to a worthy cause. We would be happy to welcome him back next year."

I felt very bad that Elayne Bennett had to waste her time defending me. But she is a stand-up woman, and she nailed the entire debacle when she said to me: "Grove took what was a great evening and turned it into something negative."

But that's what Lloyd Grove and the other witch-hunters do. They point fingers, ruin reputations, and feel darned good doing it. Predictably, Grove's dishonest column hit the special-interest websites and Fox received the usual hue and cry, demanding an apology. Grove himself appeared on MSNBC to lament the insensitivity of it all. Fanning the racial flames, he shook his head sadly at the boorishness of O'Reilly. And then, guess what: *Newsweek*, which is owned by the Washington Post Company, reprinted Grove's out-of-context quote. A perfect trifecta! The witch-hunters were delirious.

Fortunately, I have a forum where I can strike back. Fox lawyers immediately contacted the CEO of Post-Newsweek to point out that Grove's campaign was both false and malicious. I had made no racially insensitive remarks and to continue claiming otherwise could lead to legal action.

I would have made that hubcap remark to any kid with whom I was joshing around. I treat all kids the same, I don't care what color they are. To try to make a racial incident out of a simple jest is flat-out evil.

The anger I feel for the witch-hunters of America is off the charts. They come in every shape and color. The Catholic League of America issued a press release after my criticism of the Pope, charging that I "despised him." In a *Factor* segment about the Border Patrol I asked what the slang was for illegal Mexican nationals and the smugglers who lead them into the U.S.A. The words are *wetback* and *coyote*. The next day some wacked-out website said I called Mexicans "wetbacks." The hits just keep on coming.

The tragedy here is that the minority community in this country will never get the attention and resources it deserves until this kind of stuff is condemned by minority Americans themselves. As

I argue, the white majority is so afraid of being labeled and branded by the witch-hunters and racial demagogues that they often disengage from the hard analysis that can solve problems.

Gay Americans also should take note. Although there are homophobes running around, not every criticism of gays is driven by prejudice. The antics of some irresponsible homosexuals can and should be scrutinized. The out-of-control guy who luridly flaunts his homosexuality in front of children should be pilloried by all Americans, including gays. Bad conduct is bad conduct. Being a minority is not an excuse.

IN **THE END,** Americans will never come together and work out stubborn problems and attitudes if the witch-hunters are not taken down. Right now fear dominates the discussion and the bad guys are running wild. How many other TV news programs besides *The Factor* cover minority issues? How many politicians do anything more than spout platitudes?

No matter what, I will not surrender to the witch-hunters and the demagogues, because they are not looking out for anyone. They are haters. I decided this in 1975. The first major news story that I covered was the busing controversy in South Boston. A federal judge named Garrity, in an ill-conceived attempt at integration, forced little black kids to get on buses and attend school in the all-white ethnic enclave of South Boston. I saw my own people, working-class Irish-Americans, curse these young children and threaten them with harm. I saw the frightened faces of the kids and the tears in their eyes. It broke my heart. I vowed way back then that if I could right some wrongs with my reporting, I would do so. I think I've stuck to that vow.

But twenty-eight years later it is still a much tougher road for minorities in America than for us whites. Although incomes for black American couples in stable relationships are almost on a par with those of whites, the amount of grief minorities have to deal with is still far too high. But I believe most Americans are fair people. They will try to help their fellow citizens if they believe that help will be accepted in good faith. The challenge for minorities is to reject the false prophets, the racial instigators, and the phony patronizers. The system is now in place for every American to succeed if the rules of hard work, honesty, and persistence are followed. To all minority Americans, I say, don't let the white proms and the store insults affect you. Don't be misled by the haters, and above all, don't join the witch-hunters. There are people who want to look out for you, and many of them are members of the majority. They are worth seeking out.

CHAPTER NINE

Errors in Judgment

Ain't that America, somethin' to see
Ain't that America, home of the free.

—*John Cougar Mellencamp, "Pink Houses"*

THERE ARE FEW countries in the world where a guy like me, who started out with absolutely no contacts or powerful mentors, can put together a career that results in fame, influence, and financial security. In most places it simply cannot be done, and even in the U.S.A. it is rare. But, obviously, it is possible, and I am proof positive of that. So why did this happen for me? Well, among other things, I finally learned to look out for myself. Not by employing the foolish tactics of the selfish, but by mastering the art of self-protection in the pursuit of goals outside my own wants and needs.

My success is built on three foundations: personal discipline, education, and persistence. As I've written before, I am not a natural television performer. In fact, it took me years to master the skill of speaking naturally before a camera. On the other hand, I was born with verbal and writing abilities, but they lay dormant until my mid-twenties, undiscovered because no one in my life ever imagined I could make a living using them. Dissatisfied with the conventional options open to me, like teaching or law school, I pinpointed my natural abilities and figured out how to market them. Along the way there was much trial and error, but you can do the same thing. Nor does it matter how old you are. We are all born with natural talent, but we must tap into it with a vengeance in order to reach our full potential.

Here's a no-spin secret: The people you see leading the country, appearing in the media, acting on TV or in the movies, or doing anything that separates them from the crowd are usually just like you and me. I know many of them. I once sat in awe of them too. But when I finally met them up close and personal, the awe evaporated and reality set in. The so-called "stars" have the same kinds of problems the rest of us have. There is no magic that elevates their lives. They slog through the day like us—albeit with the help of publicists and hired gofers. But at night they have to shut their own eyes and dream their own dreams.

In my business, TV news, I know all the big shots. With the possible exception of Mike Wallace, who is a walking miracle, the others are simply highly skilled, highly driven men and women who capitalized on their opportunities. Brokaw, Rather, Jennings, Walters, Sawyer, and Koppel are all very smart, but they are not geniuses, nor are they the beneficiaries of any extraordinary luck. They just worked their butts off to succeed.

Throughout my television career, I never pandered to my superiors or anybody else, and this resulted in much short-term pain but even greater long-term gain. Also, I am ambitious—but never at the expense of my dignity. I never compromised my principles or stabbed anyone in the back. But here's the truly shocking truth about my success: I made so many stupid mistakes that I'd have to write three books to chronicle them.

So in the next few pages I will tell you what I did that you should *never* do. In other words, this chapter is about how to look out for yourself. We'll begin with the O'Reilly Theory of Failure: Chaos always creates more chaos. Repeat: Chaos *always* creates more chaos. Make that your mantra in life, and it will save you much heartache and failure.

Think about it in your own terms and on your own turf. I'll bet most of the disasters that have happened to you were at least in part brought on by your own poor decisions. If you marry a screwed-up person, chaos will follow. If you allow your kids to rule the house, the environment will become unbearable. If you fail to perform well at work, you will either lose your job or be made miserable by teed-off coworkers. The list goes on and on.

The antidote to chaos? Personal discipline. The ability to do the right thing most of the time will make you successful. But in addition to developing discipline, you need to keep your personal mistakes to a minimum. There is nothing more difficult in life to accomplish.

MY **MISTAKES USUALLY** were caused by a congenital impatience, insecurity, and an inability to control myself when confronted with the actions of bad people. Very often I gave my enemies all they needed to defeat me: They didn't even have to break a sweat.

At the same time, I made very few mistakes in my personal life. I have both the ability to recognize toxic people almost immediately and also the discipline to avoid them in most cases— the theme we discussed at the start of this book. I never allowed an emotionally unstable person to exploit me or lead me into destructive behavior. I was single, by choice, for decades and always chose my girlfriends carefully, treating them with respect even when things weren't going well. I took responsibility for my behavior and tried not to do anything that I thought would be harmful to me or her. And I was sober *all* the time. The result was very few dramas in my personal life and a long list of great friends, both female and male. I'm sure I disappointed some people along the way, but I tried hard to be up front and nonexploitative. I had no need for Dr. Phil, and thank God for that.

Professionally, well, that's another matter. We all make mistakes as kids, but once you reach age twenty-five you had better start to wise up. That's the age I began working at WFAA-TV in Dallas, and I was anything but wise. Previously, my experiences in journalism at Boston University (where I earned a master's degree) and at WNEP-TV in Scranton, Pennsylvania (as a rookie reporter), were generally successful. I learned the basics of my craft and did well.

But WFAA was a big-time Texas TV station with all the hyper-competitive garbage that goes along with that kind of territory. Simply put, nobody was looking out for me in the workplace, and many wanted me, a cocky Yankee, to fail dismally. So I was immediately put on the defensive, and my mistakes came fast and furious.

When a surly but powerful anchorman sneered at my clothing, I told him to f___ off. When the office-politicking assignment editor would send me on stories he knew were inconsequential, I would march into his office and demand an explanation. When a woman with minimal experience was hired to read the news, I asked why. Are you getting the picture? They disliked me at WFAA, and I not only failed to win them over, I gave them the middle digit. And I had to see these people every day!

My major weak point was insecurity. Behind my bravado, I wasn't sure if I was skilled enough to make it in television news. When I arrived in Dallas, I had been in the business for less than a year and I was still trying to prove myself to myself. Thus any criticism leveled at me stung so much that I would lash out at the messenger. Besides, I was smart enough to recognize that most of the scrutiny coming my way was mean-spirited, designed to demean me. So I fought back. Trouble was, I had no weapons.

Since that kind of situation is hardly unique to television news, you probably have experienced similar scenarios. Being pushed around while your legs are unsteady is painful, and one of the few things a person can do to relieve that pain is to talk about it with someone who is looking out for you. But I knew no one in Dallas; I had no confidants. That's when I made big mistake number one in my career. I confided in a sportscaster at the station. In hindsight, I was an idiot. The guy was scum. Everybody knew it but me. And did I ever shoot my mouth off to him, blasting others at the station who had offended me. Of course, everything I said caromed right back to the people I was lambasting. I got scorched by this guy, but I deserved it for being a fool.

The result, of course, was chaos. Almost everyone at WFAA hated me, and I was constantly under fire. To this day, some of the people I worked with in Dallas almost thirty years ago blast me whenever they can. These are generally bad people, but that's not the point. I had no idea how to deal with them, and they figuratively beat the living daylights out of me.

It took me years to learn that talking about other people in the workplace is insane; just don't do it. It is immature, doesn't solve anything, and will most always reflect poorly on you. If you don't like somebody, avoid them or confront them (always in front of witnesses). Don't bring in an unrelated third party unless it's the human resources division of the company, and make damn sure the situation is unfixable before you do that. My mistake in Dallas was not caused by malice on my part. It was born out of frustration and immaturity. But my enemies there crushed me, and I supplied the boulders.

What saved me professionally was that I performed well. I scored some touchdowns in the world of journalism. The more poorly I was treated, the more ferociously I attacked the job. I was going to *show them*. Many times I did. But because of the brutal mistakes I was making in the office, my career was much harder than it should have been. If I had just *shut up* off camera, my life would have been a lot easier.

One caveat here. You cannot allow yourself to be a doormat. Sometimes you just have to fight the louts. But remember this: To win the fight you must have allies. You must build some sort of coalition. I did not.

A**ND THAT LEADS** me to my second-biggest mistake. I was always a guy who got angry about injustice, whether social or personal. As mentioned, the best reporters and analysts are the ones who try to right wrongs. That's me, and my social conscience is a big plus in my work. My passionate crusading set me apart from the usual TV automatons. But, again, off camera I took some major hits trying to force fair play in the workplace.

In 1981, I went to work for CBS News and got royally hosed by Dan Rather and his merry men. I write about it in my book *The No Spin Zone* if you want the gory details. But the point is that I tried to convince CBS that it had an unfair system in place for the majority of its correspondents. That was like trying to convince Fidel Castro to be nicer to Cuban dissidents.

Once again, I did all the wrong things at CBS News. After coming off a good run at WCBS-TV, the local New York City station, I was way too cocky and my high opinion of myself was not shared by most of those working at the national level for CBS. They wanted me to toe the company line: "You do what we tell you to do when we tell you to do it." I have never been particularly fond of that line.

In network news there is a term called *bigfooting,* which means that a more experienced or well-known reporter is allowed to take the work of another reporter and broadcast it. This is wrong. When I was bigfooted in Argentina during the Falklands War, I instantly rebelled. A number of old CBS hands told me to let it go and be patient. But I could not discipline myself. I hit the CBS News brass head-on, telling them they were morally wrong to allow the theft of my work. Their reaction was to make an example of me by assigning me to the dismal overnight shift. The janitors and I had a great time at the CBS Broadcast Center on 57th Street.

Again, since I had no chance of winning the fight with the CBS brass, it was just plain stupid of me to mount a Light Brigade–like charge. It got me deep-sixed at the national news level, a stigma it took me years to overcome. That incident caused me more pain than anything else in my career because I knew I was good enough to report for Dan Rather, but CBS put out the word that I couldn't hack it. With an ego like mine, that kind of rap cut deep.

Five years later I got a chance to right the record at ABC News, and I did. I still didn't let the evil people push me around, but I had an ally in Peter Jennings. He looked out for me, and that made all the difference.

You see, for a very long time, in addition to being impatient, immature, and impulsive, I was clueless in the ways of social intercourse in the workplace. I was a go-it-alone type of guy, a high plains drifter who felt no need for support. I could make it by myself, I thought. Because of my upbringing, I did look out for others but never tried to find people who would look out for me. That was an enormous mistake.

I finally began to wise up about seven years into my career when Jeff Schiffman, my former boss at WCBS, saved me after the CBS debacle. After hearing about my travesty with the network, he hired me to anchor the news in Boston, where he had become a program director at the local CBS station. Schiffman is from the Bronx and doesn't buy into the corporate mentality that individuality is something to be feared. In short, he liked my street savvy and my colorful style. He literally saved my career. Without him, I would not have succeeded and you would not be reading these words today. While working with him in Boston, it dawned on me that for some reason, Jeff Schiffman was looking out for me. He really helped me when most others would not. From that time on I began to cultivate a support system. But it was a two-way street. Once I felt that a person was looking out for me, I became a soldier in their Praetorian Guard. Ask anyone who knows me. I am as loyal as I am annoying.

Anyway, that was a turning point in my professional life. By learning how to find colleagues who would look out for me, I began learning how to look out for myself. I started to develop a posse: a group of people I could call for advice and perspective. I became interested in cultivating the friendship of quality people, and that has greatly enriched my life as well as enhanced my career.

My third and final major mistake (up until this point, anyway) was to fail to anticipate what *could* happen in important situations. I pride myself on being perceptive and accurately evaluating people. In college, I loved reading the Sherlock Holmes stories because of the fictional detective's observational gifts. It is a great skill to have, and I developed my own version of it. But I left out one very important ingredient.

I often became intellectually lazy. While I saw events and people clearly, I did not carry that vision to the next step. I did not stay alert for possible betrayal. And I got hurt.

Here's a good example of my intellectual laziness. From 1989 to '95, I anchored a syndicated television program called *Inside Edition,* one of those tabloid infotainment shows, but a good one. We routinely broke national stories, and the networks copied our style in designing *Dateline, Prime Time Live,* and *48 Hours.*

I had just come off three successful years as an ABC News correspondent but knew that I had to get some national anchor experience if I wanted to take the next step and acquire some power in the industry. Unfortunately, that was not going to happen at ABC News. Although I was considered to be a solid reporter by the company, names like Stone Phillips and Forrest Sawyer, guys around my age, were getting most of the meaningful substitute anchor work.

So when *Inside Edition* offered to double my salary and appoint me both senior correspondent and exclusive substitute on the anchor desk, I left ABC for the money-driven world of syndicated television. Peter Jennings told me to my face that I was crazy, and he was probably right.

Inside Edition eventually became an enormous hit that made its owner, King World, tens of millions of dollars. But the people who ran that company had never wanted me as the anchor. I got the job by default when Sir David Frost, the original anchor, was fired three weeks into *IE*'s first year on the air. The ratings were collapsing, and King World executives were looking at a disaster of enormous proportions.

Syndicated television is even more brutal than network news, if that's possible. David Frost quickly felt the sting of that brutality and was sent on his way back to London in a hurry. The King World press release said something about Sir David doing "globe-trotting reporting" for *IE*. The truth was that the company tossed him out on his knighted posterior, and I got the call from the bullpen primarily because I was the only one in the building who could anchor the darn show.

Assuming all the writing duties, I instituted a sharp editorial focus that emphasized crusading for justice instead of gratuitous sex and violence. With the help of producers John Tomlin and Bob Young, *IE* quickly turned around and began rocketing in the ratings. Sorry if that statement doesn't sound humble, but it's the truth. The three of us took a shambles and turned it into television gold. But that wasn't good enough, because I didn't take care to look out for myself. I was too busy trying to beat *A Current Affair* and *Hard Copy* in the ratings. And we did. But along the way I got mentally flabby and stopped anticipating what might happen in the vicious world of big-time television.

There was never an easy month at *Inside Edition*. King World was constantly giving me a hard time over things like first-class airline travel and a decent publicist—perks that were givens on most other national programs. They wanted a so-called "big name" to anchor the program, so, at various points in time, the company offered my job to Mary Hart, Maury Povich, and just about everybody else in TV who could sit up straight for a half hour. My agents and I knew what was happening, but where else was I going to make that kind of money and have that kind of daily exposure? So I endured it for five years.

But in July 1994 I said, "Enough." My agent, Carole Cooper, went to King World and told them that I wanted *Inside Edition* to change into a harder-edged program with a social message. I wanted the show to take on a crusading tone and bring down some bad guys, much as *The Factor* does now.

Since the network prime-time magazines were doing what we were doing and had the personnel to do it better, I felt that *IE*'s days of prosperity were numbered unless we changed the format. I wanted to confront wrongdoing. King World wanted no part of that scenario.

So, on my instructions, my agent told King World that I would not be re-signing when my contract was up the following March and asked if, in the meantime, we could look around for other TV "opportunities." Because I was under contract, I needed permission to talk with other broadcast companies. King World came back and asked if we would keep our intentions quiet because some of the stations might be upset if I left the program, and the company wanted time to coordinate any anchor change. I agreed not to send out feelers for a new job.

Big, big mistake—and it was entirely my fault. I knew how ruthless King World was, and I fully realized they cared not a fig for me. I should have demanded the company draw up a document praising my contributions and all that stuff in return for keeping my future intentions quiet. Such letters are an important part of one's résumé in television. But I never even thought of it because I was not really looking out for myself. I was strutting around. I was even cockier than usual (if you can believe it) because the success of *Inside Edition* had dulled my instincts. I did not even consider what this company might do to me. I was a sap.

In October, I flew to Los Angeles to deliver a speech before hundreds of TV executives who had bought *Inside Edition* for their stations. The speech was a success, but immediately after it producer John Tomlin pulled me aside and told me to call my agent *right away*. The words *right away* are never good in the TV industry. Something very bad was about to happen.

Within the space of an hour, I found out that King World had hired Deborah Norville, who once had a short run on the *Today Show*, to replace me. And not only that, but the company had told a TV writer that it had fired me! Five years of hard work, a huge ratings success, and I was fired?

My surprise quickly turned to anger and then boiled over into outright rage when I read the story in the *New York Post* the next day. I was powerless to contradict the lie. But then John Tomlin stepped up and told a New York *Daily News* reporter the truth, that I had effectively resigned in July. The correct story was printed the next day.

Tomlin looked out for me, saving me a tremendous amount of heartache as well as keeping my career afloat. (Getting fired is *not* the way to TV success.) At last, I learned a very valuable lesson: In all important situations, you must stay vigilant. You must anticipate what *could* happen and take steps to prevent any dastardly deeds that may be headed your way. In hindsight, I should have never granted King World the time to do an end run—I should have negotiated the exact details of my departure, especially since I was doing them a favor by not publicly announcing my intention to move on.

And here's the kicker: Even after this debacle King World would not release me from my contract! I had to continue anchoring *Inside Edition* for six more months after the company stabbed me in the back! Can you believe it? Norville was pregnant and they didn't want to put her on the air until after she delivered. So I walked in every day, did my job, and went home with a heavy paycheck. I never could have done that earlier in my career. The Dallas-era O'Reilly would have punched somebody out. But, finally, I had developed some discipline. And, shortly after I departed, karma certainly did kick in. *Inside Edition* quickly lost ratings and influence, and Michael King, the company president and in my opinion a true villain, was forced out of his own company when King World was bought by Viacom. So there.

Trust me when I tell you that it is truly a miracle I am where I am in this world, with all the boneheaded mistakes I have made along the way. As I said, I could fill three books with them. But what's important for me and for you is to learn from self-imposed debacles. And I finally did, by learning how to look out for myself with the help of trusted advisers. And this necessary skill is critical in other aspects of your life, not just your career.

MOST AMERICANS, I believe, make most of their mistakes not in the workplace but in their personal lives. And those are even more devastating. The divorce rate in America hovers around 50 percent, and chaotic lives are on display every day, everywhere. Nobody gets away unscathed in the personal arena; at one time or another we are all victimized. But you can cut down on personal pain if you simply follow your instincts and not your heart. Repeat: Go with what you *know,* not with what you *feel*.

Here's what I mean. Most of us become infatuated with certain people over the course of our lives. Once in a while that passionate feeling works out, but much of the time it does not. Infatuation is always temporary, often based upon nothing other than powerful attraction. Unfortunately, that kind of attraction often makes us do things we would not ordinarily do. I was once infatuated with a woman who was the poster girl for venality. This woman was so selfish, she made Leona Helmsley look like Edith Bunker. She was off-the-charts manipulative and didn't even try to fake that she wasn't. She was so good-looking, she knew she could con men into giving her just about anything she wanted.

I actually thought I could change this woman. This was insane. She was disrespectful to pretty much everybody, including her parents, and openly mocked some people she had screwed over. One time she hid behind her answering machine as an old boyfriend asked her for a callback. She snorted derisively even though she had gone with the guy for years. I told her flat out that she was engaging in disgraceful behavior, but even though I knew the woman was a block of ice, I did not disengage. Looking back, she should have been lodging at the Playboy Mansion, not hanging around with me.

The good news is that I did not alter my behavior. I associated with this woman but kept my defenses up and my actions under control. Finally I wised up and told her I had better things to do with my life. However, I wasted an enormous amount of time and energy dealing with the lady, on mostly her terms. So if this can happen to me, a rather hard-edged, no-nonsense kind of guy, then it can happen to anyone.

The solution to toxic people is simple but difficult. You must divert yourself away from them. Once again it comes down to discipline. If the fruit tastes good but you bleed after eating it, you've got to dine elsewhere or be drained all the time.

What society needs is a 12-step program for infatuated Americans. This organization would supply wise counselors when we are tempted to associate with those who would do us harm but look so good doing it. I'm not kidding. If you can get somebody to come over and talk you out of making that stupid phone call to that dangerous person, do it. Then immediately go out and have some fun.

You can have plenty of good people in your life, but one emotional partner who is pernicious can negate them all. Remember, chaos always breeds more chaos. If a romantic partner (or even a family member) is causing you consistent and unnecessary pain, get out and stay out. The short-term feeling of loss is nothing compared to the damage that a truly bad or weak person can do to your life. You must see people as they are, not as you want them to be. You are not going to change a callous, cruel, selfish person.

If you do hook up with Dr. or Ms. Evil, don't blame me. I've told you the truth—you can't change him or her. Some people are bad to the bone and there's nothing anyone but the authorities can do. Learn it, live it, and spread the word.

B<small>Y **AVOIDING HURTFUL**</small> people, you are, indeed, looking out for yourself but, again, not in a selfish way. The "looking out for number one" philosophy usually involves screwing somebody over. The "looking out for yourself" philosophy makes you a more effective person, better able to help others and contribute to this world. And trying to make the world a better place is, of course, why you are here in the first place despite what the "greed is good" crowd will tell you. They are a craven, decadent bunch. Avoid them and prosper. Embrace them and suffer.

Finally, the media these days are enthralled with the words *road map,* as in President Bush's road map to Middle East peace. Another silly press cliché, but the concept of positive direction is imperative in order to have a good life. And so we will map that out in the final chapter of this book.

CHAPTER TEN

Here's to You

So let us stop talking falsely now,
The hour's getting late.

—*Bob Dylan, "All Along the Watchtower"*

MOST PEOPLE WILL not tell you the truth. Why should they? Confrontation is a hassle, and many of us tend to shoot the messenger when the news is bad. So don't expect candor, not even from those who are looking out for you. Honesty may be the best policy, but keeping one's mouth shut is the rule of the day.

For that reason, self-awareness is a must for those of us who want to fulfill our potential. Honest self-examination should be a part of our daily routine. We all make mistakes, but as we've discussed, the folks who make the fewest errors usually wind up the happiest. And there's one important corollary to self-awareness: When you do make a mistake, don't beat yourself up. I used to do that all the time. I specialized in brooding whenever I did something stupid. That meant, in my younger days, that I was brooding quite often. I developed moping into an art form.

If you are going to live a truly productive life, you have to forgive yourself. The pop psych expression for the opposite is "carrying baggage." That's another dumb cliché, but the point is that failing to recognize and accept your fallibility will lead to unhappiness; it is self-destructive to make a habit of harboring anger toward yourself. Moreover, carrying around your mistakes in an emotional knapsack will make you boring and unpleasant. Drop the guilt and strive to improve.

That takes mental discipline and self-understanding. How many people do you know who are clueless about their own behavior? Legions, I bet. But not around me. I'm the type of guy who tells people to knock it off when they become annoying. But, as I stated at the top of this chapter, most folks will not do that. They'll just avoid you instead.

Let me give you a vivid example of how clueless some people are. These days, going to the movies where I live costs ten bucks. So one night I'm sitting there during the coming attractions and this guy behind me is talking on his cell phone. I'm sure you've experienced this kind of behavior. It's the "screw you, I'll do what I want" kind of attitude. Anyway, I turn around and stare at the guy. He keeps talking. Then I get up, all six foot four of me, and say in a loud voice: "Hang that phone up or I'll take it away from you."

The guy hung up, and the theater crowd applauded. He should have been humiliated but probably wasn't. He most likely resented me for insisting on proper etiquette, but he didn't phone anyone right then to complain about it.

People like that are, unfortunately, everywhere. They probably have been poorly raised and cannot think of anyone but themselves. Combine that state of mind with poor education, and you have a potential criminal. That's how it happens.

The mind is not only a terrible thing to waste; it is also your ticket to success or failure in this life. If you never learn how to think, if you drop out of high school, if you refuse to develop your intellect by reading and engaging in serious discussions, then you will not be able to compete in modern America—unless you're lucky enough to become a rap star. I see kids all the time who are just about doomed by age sixteen because they don't know anything, and worse yet, they don't *want* to know anything. Take your mind to the mental gym every day of your life; read and think, over and over and over. It is the most important thing you can do for yourself.

Then there's your body to attend to. We all get one, and most of us abuse the heck out of it. Why? What is this all about? We pour intoxicating pollutants into our bodies, we pierce and tattoo them, we gorge on terrible food and then don't go to the doctor to gauge the damage. This is insane.

The average American alive today will live into his or her seventies. That's not a long time except to teenagers. So, from the get-go, we should be trying to maximize our time on Earth. That means staying healthy. I am simply astounded by people who smoke, drink heavily, and ingest narcotics. Millions of us are abusing the one thing we have some control over. God (or nature, for you atheists) gives you a body, a mind, and a free will. He expects you to protect the franchise.

But most of us don't. You can read nutrition and fitness books for a body primer, but remember this: Nobody can look out for you if you are a physical wreck. If you are grossly overweight or underweight, don't bathe regularly, refuse to go to the dentist, or do a myriad of other things that will hurt your body, no one can do anything for you. You will, inevitably, pay a painful price. Only the calendar date when disease pays you a visit is up in the air. So here are "looking-out-for-you" rules number one and two: Develop your mind, and respect your body.

Now THAT WE'VE settled that, I want you to meet two very powerful forces: independence and tolerance. Become acquainted with them and you will attract smart and caring people into your life.

Independence, which Americans celebrate on July 4, is not a concept that we give much thought to the rest of the year. And I'm not talking about expelling the British here. I am talking about living life without depending on somebody else to pull you along. You must become strong enough so you can go it alone if you have to. This "co-dependent" gibberish is destructive and promotes weakness.

Obviously, we all need a support system, and that is the theme of this book. But sometimes such a system, for one reason or another, is not readily available. When that happens, it's up to you to forge ahead on your own.

I learned this lesson in 1980. I was having a terrible time working at a TV station in Hartford, Connecticut. Nothing was going right, as my energetic style of presenting the news clashed with the nineteenth-century approach favored by management. I mean, we should have been wearing powdered wigs on the set! I would be out there, trying to engage the news viewer by delivering the copy with a snappy, urgent tone. Then they'd cut to my co-anchor, who was as stiff as Herman Munster. The result was disastrous, one guy reading quickly and the other somnambulant. Management quickly asked me to emulate Herman, possibly seeing me in the role of Eddie Munster.

That, of course, was not the kind of career advice I was seeking, but once again I had no one to provide perspective. I tried talking with my parents, but they seemed almost panicked at the prospect of giving their thirty-year-old son vocational guidance. My father's pithiest advice was "You can always go back to teaching."

It was then that I realized my life was my responsibility and nobody else could get me through it. My folks loved me, but they simply couldn't deal with my circumstances. They each had their own problems. So I seized the day by not heeding the bad advice my bosses were peddling. I bailed out of Hartford after only six months, but shortly after that, armed with those snappy anchor segments, I was hired by WCBS-TV in the nation's largest market: New York City.

When you become independent, you gain the freedom to work out dilemmas without having to rely on outside interference. This, in turn, raises your confidence level and helps you develop the skill of problem solving that is vital in today's complicated society. The more I overcame life's difficulties on my own, the stronger I became mentally and the more clearly I saw things. That helped me form solid relationships with people who were willing to look out for me because they knew I was able to look out for them. My success in life began accelerating, although my ego still tripped me up from time to time.

Along with developing independence, I started to flirt with tolerance. My upbringing in a working-class, all-white neighborhood had not encouraged that virtue. Outsiders were not immediately embraced in Levittown, which remains today one of the most segregated suburbs in the country. My own attitude, however, was never exclusionary. From my youngest days, I liked different kinds of people, especially those with strong points of view.

But let's face it, most Americans are uneasy with the unfamiliar, and although we are a multicultural nation, not all of us are happy about it. But I recognized that in order to succeed big in journalism, I had to communicate with and to all kinds of different people. Thus, I began to study them. And it was fascinating.

My biggest advantage in that department was that I was a dating bachelor for twenty-five years. I went out with all kinds of women, and most of them were very tolerant of me, even though often I didn't deserve it. That, in turn, taught me tolerance and also showed me that there is little difference in the basic attitudes of Americans, no matter what their ethnicity. Most will respond to a call for fairness; most harbor no permanent ill will. My life has been greatly enriched because of all the different kinds of people I have dealt with. I cringe when I hear vicious generalizations about any race.

So here's the end-zone dance on this "looking-out-for-you"

business: First, you have to be willing to see yourself honestly. Then you have to discipline yourself into cutting down on foolish mistakes. Along the way, you have to be willing to engage people whom you respect but also be willing to accept rejection. Not everyone will become your friend, but some will, and those people will make a tremendous difference for the better in your life.

Finally, stir into the mix a strong desire to develop your mind and protect your body from harm, while at the same time rewarding yourself with enjoyable times. Actively practice tolerance and build up your independent spirit. Shake things up once in a while with spontaneous fun, and you have a recipe that will keep life interesting and mostly chaos-free.

I'VE HAD A pretty good time in my life despite being a jerk on more than a few occasions. I know I've got some good people looking out for me, but I also know that when my time comes, I'll leave the world by myself. And in the end it won't matter much what President Bush did or what Bill Clinton did or even what those closest to me did. Only what *I* did will matter. How did I look out for other people? How did I conduct myself in my short time on this earth?

I fully expect to have to answer those questions to a higher power. But even if that's a myth, I still have to answer to myself. So I think I'll continue to try to look out for as many people as I can even though I concede that some may not see the method to my communicative madness. As one media analyst put it:

"O'Reilly comes off like a jerk or a genius depending on who you talk to." But I don't care about universal acceptance. The mass media are a tough game, and my approach is to lay it on the line and let the chips fall where they may, usually on somebody's head. That style is not for everyone, but, in its own way, cutting through the fog is a noble endeavor. *You* deserve to have serious issues presented with clarity so that you can evaluate them without spin. You also deserve to have a good life free of malice and tragedy. That's not always possible, but it's a worthwhile goal. And lastly, you deserve to have good people on your side.

My goal is to make the quest for those people somewhat easier. Above all, I hope I have looked out for you by writing this book. Thanks for reading it.

Acknowledgments

Writing any book is a significant challenge. The following people helped me through it: Maureen and Madeline O'Reilly, Charles Flowers, Makeda Wubneh, Eric Simonoff, Gerry Howard, Steve Rubin, Heather Maguire, John Blasi, John Carey, Bill Moser, and Russell Jones.

About the Author

Bill O'Reilly, a two-time Emmy Award winner for excellence in reporting, is a twenty-year veteran of the television industry. He served as national correspondent for ABC News and as anchor of the nationally syndicated newsmagazine program *Inside Edition* before joining Fox News Channel, where he is currently executive producer and anchor of his own prime-time news program, *The O'Reilly Factor*. The author of the huge best-sellers *The O'Reilly Factor* and *The No Spin Zone,* as well as the novel *Those Who Trespass,* he holds a master's degree in public administration from Harvard's Kennedy School of Government and a master's degree in broadcast journalism from Boston University.